HOUSES OF MEXICO

Origins and Traditions

Immediately beyond the foyer of Seville's *Alcázar* this window, overlooking a paved *patio*, is protected by an iron grille with bouyant cresting of elongated scrolls and flowers, springing from here and there, topped by a symbol of the Trinity. The grating with its split heart is a prototype of many splendid *rejas* in Mexico.

HOUSES
of
MEXICO

ORIGINS AND TRADITIONS

Verna Cook Shipway and Warren Shipway

ARCHITECTURAL BOOK PUBLISHING COMPANY

TAYLOR TRADE PUBLISHING
Lanham • New York • Boulder • Toronto • Plymouth, UK

Architectural Book Publishing Company
Published by Taylor Trade Publishing
An imprint of The Rowman & Littlefield Publishing Group, Inc.
4501 Forbes Boulevard, Suite 200, Lanham, Maryland 20706
www.rlpgtrade.com

Estover Road, Plymouth PL6 7PY, United Kingdom

Distributed by National Book Network

The Architectural Book Publishing edition of this book was previously catalogued
by the Library of Congress. Catalog Card Number: 72-133125

ISBN: 978-1-58979-643-0 (pbk. : alk. paper)
ISBN: 978-1-58979-644-7 (electronic)

∞™ The paper used in this publication meets the minimum requirements of
American National Standard for Information Sciences—Permanence of Paper
for Printed Library Materials, ANSI/NISO Z39.48-1992.

Printed in the United States of America

CONTENTS

Foreword....................IX

Picture Locations....................XI

Glossary....................XVII

ARCHES, ARCADES....................36, 37, 40, 95, 97, 157, 159, 163, 244, 245

BALCONIES, RAILINGS, BALUSTRADES....................55, 56, 57, 101, 183, 206, 207, 208, 210

BEDS....................173, 190, 191, 192, 194, 195, 196, 197, 198, 199, 200, 215

BEDROOMS, BATHS....................116, 117, 130, 131, 142, 172, 173, 194, 195

CABAÑAS, CABANAS, SWIMMING POOLS....................4, 84, 85, 86, 87, 91, 92, 96, 97, 168, 243

CABINETS, VARGUEÑOS, WRITING DESKS, TABLES....................9, 64, 80, 106, 119, 121, 145, 148

CARVING — STONE & WOOD....................6, 15, 16, 17, 39, 81, 89, 127, 166, 171, 211, 238, 239

CEILINGS, DECORATIVE PLASTER, CUPOLAS....................41, 49, 50, 52, 54, 63, 79, 125, 139, 144, 167, 186, 216, 219

CHAIRS, BENCHES, OTTOMANS....................17, 70, 71, 72, 73, 74, 75, 77, 126, 145, 146, 147

V

Contents

CHESTS and THEIR HARDWARE 116, 149, 150, 151, 233

CHIMNEYS, WEATHERVANES.............. 32, 33, 34, 35

CRISTOS, SANTOS, RELIGIOUS OBJECTS..............42, 62, 88, 90, 126, 140, 141, 142, 172, 188, 203

DINING ROOMS..............10, 16, 29, 61, 79, 171, 202, 216, 227

DOORS, CANCELAS..............18, 19, 60, 134, 135, 211, 214, 218

ENTRANCE COURTS, PAVING.............. 2, 12, 112, 124, 137, 165, 174, 175, 176, 177, 178, 179

ENTRANCE FEATURES..............20, 21, 43, 123, 156, 160, 232

FAÇADES..............26, 37, 40, 100, 102, 164, 168, 240

FIESTA CHARACTERS..............68, 239

FIREPLACES..............11, 30, 61, 63, 66, 85, 86, 87, 115, 122, 138, 189, 193, 203, 213, 226, 227, 235

FOYERS, GALLERIES, PASSAGEWAYS, ZAGUÁNS..............8, 15, 50, 77, 78, 103, 123, 133, 186

FRESCOES..............44, 45, 48

GARDEN WALLS, POOLS 4, 40, 82, 89, 90, 93, 94, 158, 161

GATES, GRILLES.............. Frontispiece, 22, 23, 24, 25, 76, 84, 100, 103, 112, 113, 182, 209, 224, 240, 248

LANTERNS, LAMPS, CHANDELIERS.............. 76, 78, 94, 105, 107, 108, 109, 110, 111, 122, 152, 153, 170, 223

LOGGIAS, CORREDORES, TERRACES..............3, 4, 38, 59, 67, 96, 166, 167, 174

MIRRORS, FRAMES..............1, 9, 64, 131, 184, 185

PAINTINGS, TROMPE de l'OEIL 46, 47, 58, 63, 65, 78, 145, 154, 155, 187, 202, 207

PAPIER-MÂCHÉ..............68, 69, 152, 224, 229

PATIOS, FOUNTAINS..............51, 53, 81, 104, 105, 158, 174, 180, 181, 188

POTTERY — PRE-HISPANIC, TALAVERA, & OTHER..............30, 114, 128, 129, 130, 136, 154, 158, 165, 189, 232, 243, 249

PRE-HISPANIC FLAT STAMPS..............96, 102, 248

RUGS, FABRICS, WALL HANGINGS 31, 66, 157, 220, 221, 222, 223

SALAS, ESTANCIAS..............14, 29, 39, 66, 73, 122, 125, 139, 212, 213, 225, 233

SCREENS, DECORATIVE ACCESSORIES..................61, 118, 120, 147, 153, 170, 198, 205, 211, 217

SCULPTURE — METAL 12, 90, 114, 115, 130, 162, 182, 246

STAIRWAYS..................6, 7, 55, 56, 57, 77, 133, 139, 204, 206, 207, 208, 234

STUDIES, STUDIOS, KITCHENS..................11, 80, 82, 143, 188, 228, 236

THATCHING, SUNSHADES..................242, 243

TILES..................30, 82, 83, 115, 126, 130, 131, 132, 133, 156, 228, 236

TRIVIA..................201, 220, 238

WALLS — PLAIN, ORNAMENTED, PIERCED & GLAZED..................28, 76, 98, 99, 161, 170, 230, 231, 247

WALLS — PRE-HISPANIC..................31, 246

FOREWORD

"As the Italians sing and Frenchmen cook, Mexicans relish making things. The universal yen for beauty in visual form is taken for granted to be a need as natural as love and as ancient and accessible as frijoles. It proliferates in everything from the carefully made arrangements of color and form in the fruit and vegetable markets to the daring of entire buildings covered with mosaic murals."

ANITA BRENNER
"A Critic's View"

THIS CREATIVE genius had its earliest roots in a nebulous background of impressions and fancies. Legendary pottery figurines, massive sculptures, incised hieroglyphs in stone, picture-writings of codices record a mix of brilliant civilizations and master artists. It was further shown by ritual dances propitiating their favored deities — the Sun, the Moon, the Rain God. Fantastic masks, painted faces, regional costumes at times gorgeously colored and feathered, joined the swirl of motifs and symbols.

While one after another Indian peoples presumably starting with the Mayas, brought their highly developed cultures to fruition, Spain was under the domination of the Moors from North Africa. Deeply implanted throughout the Iberian Peninsula was the latter's manner of living. The family was treasured, protected and veiled; the home inward-looking with few openings in outside walls guarded by iron grilles. The patio, enhanced by its murmur of falling water, was a center of activities but, in turn, only vaguely seen from the outside through delicate openwork screening. So deeply rooted and so favored became this mode of life, transplanted by the Conquistadores and their followers into New Spain, that it persists today, in plan and in spirit if not under such rigidity.

Meanwhile, into the western ports of México were sifting Oriental and Chinese flavors. As objects were unloaded and repacked on burros for the long trek eastward to Veracruz on the Gulf coast bound for Spanish ports, they left in their wake the spice and subtlety of color and curve of Asian arts.

Through Spain came influences from other European countries: seafaring ventures of Portugal brought exotic decorative elements; Flanders, during its temporary control by Spain, introduced a primitive, provincial quality frequently including the bulbous vase-shaped turning. And from England came furniture with flowing lines, ample proportions and accenting the scallop-shell motif, which appeared to mesmerize the export trade of the Queen Anne era.

These mannerisms, modes of living and design patterns we call the traditions. Today a surge backward brings into the bosom of progress the images of the pre-Hispanic. Juan O'Gorman contends that "Mexicans must find their roots among the pre-Columbian Gods or perish in the faceless maelstrom of modernism".

PICTURE LOCATIONS

MÉXICO

ACCESORIOS en Decoración, México, D.F.: 147

ALHÓNDIGA de Granaditas, Guanajuato, Gto.: 30, 68, 136, 141

ALONSO Arturo, Cuernavaca, Mor.: 48, 86

       Arturo Alonso, Architectural Designer and Jesús Sanchez, Engineer

APARTMENT Building, Mexico, D.F.: 248

       Leonardo Zeevaert, Engineer and Consultant

ARELLANO Humberto Garza, near Monterrey, N.L.: 63, 84, 85, 87, 131

       Humberto Arellano Garza, Designer

BAROCIO Marco Aurelio, Ing., and Helga Martens de, Puebla, Pue.: 76, 77, 78, 79, 80, 81, 82, 131

       Ing. Marco Aurelio Barocio, Architectural Designer

BARNES Paul, San Miguel de Allende, Gto.: 197

       Paul Barnes, Architectural Designer

BARRIGA Miguel Díaz, Ing., Puebla, Pue.: 122, 123, 124, 125, 126, 127

BAZAR de los Sapos, Puebla, Pue.: 50, 51, 52, 53, 54, 55, 72, 129, 132, 146

BELLOLI Giorgio and Louise, Marfil near Guanajuato, Gto.: 42, 48, 89, 145

       Giorgio Belloli, Architectural Designer

BORISOV Saul, San Angel Inn, México, D.F.: 220, 221, 222

BURKHOLDER John, Marfil near Guanajuato, Gto.: 189

       Giorgio Belloli, Architectural Designer

CARÁPAN, Monterrey, N.L.: 158, 182

CARLETON Horace and Florence Noyes, Tlaltinango near Cuernavaca, Mor.: 25, 94, 95, 96, 97

    Florence Noyes Carleton, Architect

CASA de las Artesanias de Jalisco, Guadalajara, Jal.: 83, 184

CASA del Balam, Mérida, Yuc.: 108, 196, 244

CASITA of Arturo Alonso, Cuernavaca, Mor.: 182

    Arturo Alonso, Architectural Designer and Jesús Sanchez, Engineer

CENTRO Regional de la Artesanias y el Folklore, Puebla, Pue.: 68, 88, 129, 239

CHAPA Pedro y Sra., Cuernavaca, Mor.: 90

CHÁVEZ-MORADO José and Olga Costa, Guanajuato, Gto.: 137, 138, 139, 140, 142, 143

    José Chávez-Morado, Designer

CHAVOLLA Samuel, Apaseo el Grande, Gto.: 159

CHURCH of La Portada de la Capilla del Rosario, Querétaro, Qro.: 160

CHURCH of San Bautista, Zimapan, Hgo.: 49

CHURCH of San Jerónimo, Tlacochahuaya, Oax.: 43, 44, 45

COTÉ Ray, Santa Maria Hills, Mich.: 64, 65, 197, 199

    Ray Coté, Architectural Designer

CUSI Francisco, Las Lomas, México, D.F.: 148

    Rodolfo Ayala, Architectural Designer

DAVILA, Marcial, Cuernavaca, Mor.: 113

DREIER Theodore, Guanajuato, Gto.: 74, 91

    Giorgio Belloli, Architectural Designer

DUPUIS Roberto and Georgina, Pedregal de San Angel, México, D.F.: 47

ELLIS Allen and Dorothy, Cuernavaca, Mor.: 46, 116, 117, 118, 119, 176

    Rodolfo Ayala, Architectural Designer

EMAÚS S.A., México, D.F.: 12, 114, 115, 130, 246

EX-CONVENTO de los Siete Príncipes, Oaxaca, Oax.: 23, 102, 144

EXHIBITION Palacio de las Bellas Artes, México, D.F.: 162

    Mathias Goeritz, Sculptor

FERNANDEZ Dr. Virgilio and Gene Byron de, Marfil near Guanajuato, Gto.: 110, 232, 233, 234, 235, 236, 237

    Gene Byron de Fernandez, Designer

GALERÍA "Trini", Cuernavaca, Mor.: 69, 149

GARCÍA Francisco Valencia, San Miguel de Allende, Gto.: 87, 109, 132, 192, 193
        Francisco García Valencia, Architectural Designer

GIFT SHOP, Hotel Victoria, Oaxaca, Oax.: 201
        José Velasco, Designer and Fabricator

GORDON Lena, Tlaltinango near Cuernavaca, Mor.: 58, 59
        Rodolfo Ayala, Architectural Designer

HACIENDA de Buena Vista, near Chapala, Jal.: 21

HACIENDA Chenku, Mérida, Yuc.: 36, 37, 38, 39, 40, 41

HACIENDA San Pedro, near Mérida, Yuc.: 163, 245

HAUGH John and Emily, Valenciana near Guanajuato, Gto.: 102, 103, 104, 105, 106, 194
        Giorgio Belloli, Architectural Designer

HOLBERT Matilde, Cuernavaca, Mor.: 132
        Rodolfo Ayala, Architectural Designer

HOTEL El Camino Real, México, D.F.: 49, 75, 161
        Ricardo Legorreta Vilchis, Architect

HOTEL Hacienda Chichén, Chichén Itzá, Yuc.: 157

HOTEL Hacienda Uxmal, Uxmal, Yuc.: 243

HOTEL Instituto Allende, San Miguel de Allende, Gto.: 26

HOTEL Jurica Querétaro, near Querétaro, Qro.: 164, 165, 166, 167, 168, 169, 170, 171, 172, 173, 174
        José Chávez-Morado, Designer

HOUSE in Oaxaca, Oax.: 183

HOUSES in Mérida, Yuc.: 240, 241

JOHNSON J.B., México, D.F.: 151, 186, 187, 188
        J.B. Johnson, Architect

LANDA Juan José Torres, San José Iturbide, Gto.: 26, 27, 28, 29, 30, 48

LEIGH Howard, Mitla, Oax.: 249

MACDONALD Dorothy, Taxco, Gro.: 74
        William Spratling, Architect

MEZZANINE SHOP, México, D.F.: 61, 152, 153

MILLER Thomas Briscoe, Coyoacán, Mexico, D.F.: 135

MOSER Henry and Freda, Cuernavaca, Mor.: 92, 133, 134, 178
        Rodolfo Ayala, Architectural Designer

MUÑOZ Rivera José Trinidad, Tlaltinango near Cuernavaca, Mor.: 238
    Rodolfo Ayala, Architectural Designer
MUSEO de la Cerámica, Tlaquepaque, al.: 114
MUSEO de Jorge Wilmot, Tonalá, Jal.: 155
    Jorge Wilmot, Designer
MUSEO Nacional de Antropologia, México, D.F.: 247
MUSEO Nacional de Artes e Industrias Populares, México, D.F.: 68, 130, 154, 189
MUSEO del Virreinato, Tepotzotlán, Méx.: 93
OAXACA Cathedral, Oaxaca, Oax.: 19
OLIVIER Jean-Paul, Las Lomas, México, D.F.: 208, 210
    Jean-Paul Olivier, Designer
OVANDO Carlos de and Carmen Peréz de Salazar de, Las Lomas, México, D.F.:
    120, 121, 129
PANI Arturo and BALLENGER Edward, Acapulco, Gro.: 1, 2, 3, 4, 5, 6, 7, 8, 9,
    10, 11, 153
    Arturo Pani, Interior Architect and Decorator and Edward Ballenger,
    Landscape Architect
PARADOR San Javier, Guanajuato, Gto.: 60, 61
PATRIC'S Arts and Crafts Shop, Mérida, Yuc.: 157
PEON Pedro M. de Regil, Mérida, Yuc.: 73, 179, 202
    Fernando Roche M., Engineer
PONCE Pedro and Lia, Mérida, Yuc.: 203, 204, 205
    Felix Mier y Teran, Architectural Designer
PRIETO Eduardo Lopez, Lic., Pedregal de San Angel, México, D.F.: 13, 14, 15,
    16, 17
    Luis Barragán, Architect
RUINS Mitla, Oax.: 31
RUINS Uxmal, Yuc.: 246
SACRISTY Church of San Juan, Mérida, Yuc.: 245
SALA de Artes, México, D.F.: 72, 111, 146, 200, 201, 223
SARGENT Cynthia, México, D.F.: 220
SCHLEE Charles G. and Jeanne Valentine, San Miguel de Allende, Gto.: 224, 225,
    226, 227, 228, 229
    Nicolas Schlee, Architect

SNYDER Oliver and Dorcas, San Miguel de Allende, Gto.: 180
STODDARD Frances, San Miguel de Allende, Gto.: 181, 198
TEIXIDOR Felipe, Cuernavaca, Mor.: 135
      Fendall Gregory, Architect
TURNER Joseph and Viola, Pedregal de San Angel, México, D.F.: 108, 130, 147,
      211, 212, 213, 214, 215, 216, 217, 218
      Rodolfo Ayala, Architectural Designer
VILLA MONTAÑA, Santa Maria Hills, Morelia, Mich.: 70, 71, 239
      Ray Coté, Architectural Designer
WALL Oaxaca, Oax.: 230
WHITEHOUSE Robert and Dorothy, Cuernavaca, Mor.: 196
      Rodolfo Ayala, Architectural Designer
WILSON David M. and Anne, San Miguel de Allende, Gto.: 22, 158, 195, 206, 207
      Casas Coloniales, Construction and Decoration
WYNKOOP Henry, Taxco, Gro.: 66, 67, 152
YALALAG SHOP, Oaxaca, Oax.: 31, 238

PORTUGAL

ESPLANADE, Figuerira da Foz: 177
HOUSES in the Algarve, Évora and Fátima: 32, 33, 34, 35
HOUSES in Ericeíra: 156
MUSEO Nacional de Machado Castro, Coimbra: 34, 35
NATIONAL University, Coimbra: 20, 57, 231
POUSADA dos Lóios, Évora: 190
WALL near Obidos: 98, 99

SPAIN

ALCÁZAR, Córdoba: 182
ALCÁZAR, Seville: Frontispiece, 108, 112, 209, 219
ALFAR de la MENORA, Talavera de la Reina: 128
BEACH, Formentor, Majorca: 242
CASA Raimoro, Ronda: 191
HOSTEL del Cardinal (Botin's), Toledo: 18, 185

Picture Locations

HOUSE in Córdoba: 101
HOUSE in San Fernando: 100
HOUSE in Seville: 24, 209
HOUSE in Ubeda: 135
HOUSES in Palma, Majorca: 56, 57
MUSEO Provincial de Belles Artes, Córdoba: 175
PARADOR de Nerja, near Malaga: 114, 115, 177
PARADOR de Oropesa, Oropesa: 122, 219
PARADOR Nacional Condestable Davalos, Ubeda: 107
PARADOR Nacional de Mérida, Mérida: 110

GLOSSARY

Italicized Spanish words appearing in the captions are defined below.

ALABRIJAS.................a combination of two words, LEGATIJA, meaning 'lizard' and BRUJA, meaning 'witch'.

ALBERCA.................swimming pool

ALCÁZAR.................fortress, castle or royal palace

ALHÓNDIGA DE GRANADITAS.................a former seed and grain warehouse, now a museum.

ANDAS.................portable platforms used to carry religious figures

AZUL.................blue

AZULEJO.................glazed tile

BANDIDO.................bandit, gangster

BAROQUE.................term used today for art style, period 1600 to 1720. Originally from "barroco" meaning irregularly shaped pearl, and used to describe the ornate and bizarre. An outgrowth of Renaissance, originating in Rome. After its transplanting by the Spanish to their American Colonial empire, the Baroque became a true architectural style of the New World.

BAZAR DE LOS SAPOS.................an antique shop in Puebla on the Square of the Toads.

BODEGA................storage room

BRASERO................cooking top, masonry with gas or charcoal

BUTACA................classic armchair of México

CABALLERO............gentleman, horseman

CABAÑA................cabin, hut

CABANA................bath house

CAMBAYA................fine cotton cloth

CANCELA................screening door from zaguán to patio

CANTERA................quarry stone

CASA DE ALFEÑIQUE................a former mansion used as a residence for visiting high dignitaries as they traveled between the Gulf coast and the Capital, now a museum: "Sugar Cake House".

CASA DE LA CÚPULA................original name of the early residence now housing Bazar de los Sapos.

CASA DE LAS ARTESANIAS DE JALISCO................museum of, and sales outlet for, the State of Jalisco popular arts, Guadalajara

CASA DEL BALAM................house of the "tiger" or "leading spirit"; home of the late Fernando Barbachano Peón

CENTRO REGIONAL DE LAS ARTESANIAS Y EL FOLKLORE................museum of Puebla State popular arts in Puebla

CHENKU (or CHEN-KU)................in the phonetics of the original inhabitants, "place of any one of several wild animals".

CHICHÉN-ITZÁ................in Mayan, "edge of the well of the Itzaes".

CHIHUAHUENSE................product of Chihuahua, Chih.

CHURRIGUERESQUE................a peculiarly Spanish outcome of the Baroque style, the utmost in architectural unrestraint and wondrous intricacy. Named after José Churriguera, Spanish architect (about 1660-1725).

CITARILLA................open fence

COMEDOR................dining room

CONQUISTADORES................conquerors of New Spain

CORREDOR................gallery around a patio

CUADRÁNGULO de las MONJAS................nunnery quadrangle of Uxmal

DANZA................dance

DIEZMO................tithe

"ESTA ES SU CASA"................a phrase of hospitality meaning "Consider this house your home".

ESTANCIA................room

ESTÍPITE................ pilaster in form of an inverted pyramid, characteristically Churrigueresque

GALERÍA................gallery

GESSO................Plaster of Paris or gypsum used to form a smooth coating on which to paint

HACENDADO................owner of a hacienda

HACIENDA .... estate, large farm, income-producing property

HAMACA................hammock

ING.................abbreviated form of "ingeniero" meaning "engineer"

JURICA................"place of witch doctor"

LATÓN................brass

LIC. ....abbreviated form of "licenciado" meaning lawyer

LLAMADOR................door knocker

MAESTRO................master craftsman

MANTILLA................ Spanish veil or scarf for the head

MARIACHIS................ strolling folk orchestras

MEDIO-PAÑUELO................ one-half handkerchief

MESA de MOLER................ a table to hold metates

METATE................ a flat stone on which corn is ground

MUDÉJAR................style of architecture or art in the Christian parts of Spain in which Moorish and Italian Renaissance details were seen in the same design.

MULETA................red cloth draped over sword used by bullfighters

MUSEO................museum

NAHUAL................ a mythical Aztec being with power of transforming itself into an animal, when bent on mischief

OBELISCO................obelisk

PADRE................father

PÁJARO................bird

PALAPA .... leaf of tree palm used for thatching; any small thatched shelter or arbor

XIX

PARADOR................Spanish inn, now applied to the handsome, government operated lodgings

PASTITA or PASTITLAN................Indian meaning "place of grasses"

PATIO................open court, inner courtyard

PIÑATA................a decorated clay jar filled with small toys and candies to be broken by a blindfolded person during a fiesta

PISO BAJO................ground or street floor

POSTIGO................small opening or panel in a door of larger size

POTENCIA................power, potency, three groups of rays symbolic of the Father, the Son, and the Holy Ghost

POUSADA................a Portuguese inn similar to the Spanish parador

QUIMERA................an imaginery protective monster

RAMILLETE................bouquet, flower cluster, also known as "palmerine", a candle shield of tin or brass with short candle holder on back

RANA................frog

REJA................grating, grille

SABINO................water cypress of México, "Arbol de la Noche Triste"

SALA................formal room, parlor

SANTO -TA................image of a saint

SIRENA................mermaid

SOL CABELLO LARGO................name applied to Emaús metal sculpture meaning "long haired sun"

TABURETE................stool, footstool

TALAVERA................glazed pottery made in Puebla, México, similar to that made in Talavera de la Reina, Spain, while under Spanish domination; now continuing in a more colorful, native character

TALLER................workshop, atelier

TEPETATE................white marlaceous substance, almost hard as cement when exposed to air

TORRE................tower

TÚNEL................enclosed passageway

VARGUEÑO................Spanish cabinet and desk with a drop-lid

VIGA................beam, girder

ZAGUÁN................open passageway through house to patio

ZEMPASUCHITL................marigold flower, the "flower of the dead"

HOUSES OF MEXICO
Origins and Traditions

A double-headed, crowned eagle, the 16th century emblem of Charles I of Spain while also Charles V of the Holy Roman Empire, Emperor of Flanders, Austria and Germany. Here a Mexican reproduction of the 17th century Spanish original, richly carved and gold leafed, encloses an octagonal mirror.

Acapulco reflects
the Mediterranean

Inside a walled street-entry, this circular court, paved with river pebbles embedded in white cement, is surrounded by tropical greenery. The generous flight of stairs on the left curves upward to the entrance door behind a vine covered parapet wall: the home of Arturo Pani and Edward Ballenger.

At the end of the open passageway on the preceding page with its regimented potted shrubs, the door communicating with the service is completely mirror-covered. In addition to giving the illusion of doubled length to the passage, one unexpectedly seems to grect oneself upon entering the home, a quite unusual experience.

On a spacious terrace with uninterrupted views of magnificent Acapulco Bay, Arturo Pani and Edward Ballenger have contrived a veritable utopia. Opposite the start of the stair on Page 7, double oak doors 12 feet tall open on a palm court enclosed by an even higher treillage. At its far end a small ball-like fountain flanked by two old majolica busts on pedestals, plays into a shallow pool connected with the *alberca* above.

The court and partially shaded pool-side lounging area are paved with large, pre-cast panels of light oatmeal-colored concrete, delicately peened after laying, giving texture to their surfaces. White furniture, bamboo, wicker, and steel and the white trellis of open concrete lozenges, reflected in the shimmering pool, all crisply contrast with the vibrant greens of the foliage against the blues of the sky.

4

Finished in a mellow light brown, an armless wood statue arises from the heavy, variegated dark-green leaves. Above, cantilevered cement treads are skillfully formed with splayed undersides increasing in depth at the wall for added strength. The ever-changing play of light and shade upon their several surfaces gives the illusion of magic.

At midpoint of the entrance gallery, the adjoining stair-well terminates in a sky-light. Beyond open treads lies the *comedor* with its clipped hedge and semi-circular breakfast terrace. Above tropical palms, a model galleon in memory of Acapulco's early trade with the Far East, is a central feature on the dark-stained, adzed fascia.

7

Turning to the left inside the front entrance, a vista extends to the Pacific's horizon. Under stippled, sand-colored ceilings, gleaming Carrara marble floors covering the *piso bajo*, lead past the cantilevered stair and lush planting into the *sala* beyond.

Contrasting with the prevalent white walls, a short partition of antiqued wood is introduced. It serves as the background for the mirror, framed in dark red with gold leaf motifs and an old French Provincial dough-table with its becoming ornaments.

9

From the breakfast terrace, this polished, refreshing dining area is dominated by the luminous crystals of the French chandelier and duplicate Page 1 mirrors on opposite walls. Circled by Italian Provincial chairs of modified Queen Anne style, the table top is decorated with an attenuated star in muted colors, glazed so skillfully it appears inlaid.

Intimacy and charm, innate in provincial, neo-classic interiors of France during the late 1700's, are echoed in a softly colored library. With simplicity as keynote, rococo curves having been discarded, symmetry is here accented by a gros-point rug, designed and embroidered by Mr. Ballenger, offsetting the black slate floor.

Home of Arturo Pani and Edward Ballenger

Within a flaming sun, 29 inches in diameter, Sol-dos-Caras, the profiles of a man and woman in sheet-iron repoussé are representative of life, love, and completeness. After submergence in a special *latón* bath, the effect of rich, Roman gold is scintillating.

In two small buildings, part of the former monastery on the hills north and west of Cuernavaca, young ex-postulants of the Benedictine order continue this creative work in metals under the direction of Grégoire Lemercier. Their products bearing the name EMAÚS, an ancient Biblical town, are unique.

truly, a
deeply-rooted
mexican house

Built before 1950, this seemingly monumental
construction is the home of *Lic*. Eduardo Prieto
Lopez. Designed by Luis Barragán, it was one of
the earliest of the remarkable grouping of homes
which occupy an ancient lava flow now known as
"Jardines del Pedregal". Here, facing the courtyard, unadorned walls cast heroic shadows.

A corner of the spacious *sala*: off-white walls of majestic height overlook mustard-colored shag carpeting. On the cupboard, a small archangel and delicate iron candleholder with moulded Swedish glass drops are both accented against a panel of gold leaf. Outside, wooden horses prance by.

On a parapet wall rising above the half-flight of stairs from an impressive reception hall stands, at the focal point, an arresting wood statue of a winged angel, carved by Mathias Goeritz.

Rational and logical in this generously proportioned home is the use of sturdy furniture of simple design. Walls without doors separate the several major rooms.

Left: Surrounded by extensive grounds on several levels and numerous crannies, a grassed upper terrace with its fountain, statuary, and old trees provides entrancing vistas from *sala* and *comedor*.

The dramatic angel now silhouetted against an unadorned background while the curved legs of four aligned ottomans form a flattened guilloche pattern to swing across the foreground.

Above, a richly studded and massive old door at the entrance to Hostel del Cardinal within walled Toledo, Spain.

Opposite: Contrasting in marked simplicity are the doors of Oaxaca's 17th century cathedral. The carved, green stone band furnishes needed counterpoint.

Facing the quadrangle overlooked by the former royal palace on Page 57, this entrance is an excellent example of the Manuelino period (1495-1521), a name for the Gothic phase of minutely scaled superabundance with strong East Indian influences.

In a lower wing of the owner's home, Hacienda de Buena Vista at Ixtlahuacan de los Membrillos near Chapala, this captivatingly rare interpretation of a scroll pediment frames an entrance to the lodge office. Below an iron balustrade, the warm white wall is a fitting background for the delicacy of light, greenish-gray, native stone carvings.

Home of David M. and Anne Wilson

Near the *alberca*, a small open-beamed refreshment area lies at the foot of the masonry stairs leading to the Guest House through fan-topped, iron gates.

22

Modern iron screens of novel pattern fill the several interior archways of a refurbished old monastery providing security, ventilation and light for upper offices.

Ex-Convento de los Siete Príncipes

Included in this majestic wrought-iron grille is a gate under the classic curved transom which leads to the unroofed entrance foyer of a Seville home. The surrounding wall, decorated with tile and golden panels in low relief, is remarkable for the diversity of its many motifs.

24

Imported from France during the short reign of Maximilian and Carlota, the elegant cast iron gate leads from the pool patio on Page 94 to the service and utility passage as shown on the Carleton plan. It is flanked by short sections of *citarillas* similar to one adjoining the nearby old church of San Jerónimo.

Home of the Horace Carletons

Instituto Allende

state seal of Guanajuato

"el Diezmo"

Left: Seen across terraced lawns, the double-barrel, roofed granary of the old *Diezmo* looms above added wings. For many years, these vast halls were used by the local church as a warehouse for the storage of its communicants' varied tithes.

Later a school, it is now the home of *Lic.* Juan José Torres Landa, the former governor of the State of Guanajuato responsible for, among other improvements, the pictorial entry and passage under the city of Guanajuato.

An imposing buttress with pillowed heading, decorative as well as structural, braces the end wall alongside the arched vehicle entrance at the southerly end of this old building.

28

Intimacy has been gained for the slightly over fifteen foot wide *sala* and distant *comedor* by the insertion of beams below the thirty-five foot high arched ceiling.

Home of Juan José Torres Landa

With a changing play of light from above, the beams cast ripples of shadows on white walls, at the moment less defined here over the *sala's* spacious fireplace. Below a heavy wood mantel, the pink *cantera* hearth has a riser faced with *medio-pañuelo* patterned tile.

Left: A group of pre-Hispanic figures in the *Alhóndiga* collection of Chávez-Morado would seem to be singing a welcome to the ceramic members of another culture on the mantel.

South-east of Oaxaca are the ruins of Mitla, known to the Aztecs of the 16th century as Mictlan, "a place of sadness". Although this ancient city was built by Zapotec Indians centuries before its discovery by the *Conquistadores*, the mosaics on some of its walls are today much as they were over 400 years ago. Rectangular stone blocks, 6″ thick, cut back 1″ as necessary to form the various stepped-fret designs, were accurately fitted and embedded in the surfaces of the 4 to 5 foot thick masonry walls. *Right:* The black and off-white wool rug evidences the continuing popularity of the designs above.

some vanes and chimneys of Portugal

Except for that opposite in Fátima and at the lower right on the following page in Évora, all other chimneys are in the "Florida" of Portugal, a 100 mile strip along its southern coast. The area is known as the Algarve, a corruption of the old Moorish name Al-Gharb, meaning the West.

33

Gallos de Viente or weathercocks, above and opposite, now guard the entrance to the Museo Nacional de Machado Castro near Portugal's ancient university established in Coimbra since 1307. *Right:* A massive Évora chimney is typical of its region.

These fanciful chimney tops remindful of domed mosques and delicate minarets are found throughout the Algarve. The one above of tile and cement-covered brick, all painted white, proudly stands above the recently constructed home of a railroad gate keeper.

Chenku: an old henequén hacienda

Hacienda of Guy Puerto P. and José Palomeque C.

A joyous welcome is extended by the proud yet spontaneous Mérida gateway on the opposite page. Are not its outlines enclosing a *mudéjar* arch remindful of Oriental influences introduced by the Portuguese?

Located only a short distance away is the *hacienda* owner's residence. Its arcaded façade, over 100 feet long, was built during two periods. The original section of the home with the small belfry over the wide arch, has a long extension to the rear. Completed in the 18th century, the subsequent 19th century addition toward the left made a major contribution to its present air of distinction.

Facing north behind the arcade on the preceding page, a stone floored loggia is characteristic of a Yucatán outdoor living area; it avoids the sun and enjoys the breezes. A finely woven example of the ubiquitous *hamaca* (here an extra wide matrimonial hammock) is hung from one of the many wall hooks to a column. The crude, old table holding *metates*, is known as a *"mesa de moler"*. With its carved back rail, the long bench is from an 18th century Oaxaca convent.

Between two protected exterior walls, the *sala*, a part of the original Chenku main house, was designed for coolness. Over a recently constructed fireplace, is an unusual 18th century wood portrait of San José from the private chapel of another *hacienda*. His right hand is freestanding while his head and body, draped in flowing robes, are carved in strong relief from thick mahogany planks.

The word *Chenku* or *Chen-ku* in the phonetics of the early Indians was a speech sound. Depending on its intonation it meant "the place of" any one of several local wild animals.

The westerly approach through that fanciful gate on Page 36 has been abandoned. The present southerly drive ends at this raised grass terrace, its pool spotted with water lilies. Separating the exterior wall, vibrant with bougainvillea, two loggias with white arches and inner walls have ceilings similar to that opposite.

Shallow plastered brick arches spacing crudely-cut rafters supported by heavy *vigas* produce a pleasing homespun effect.

42   A realistic and sorrowful figure of Christ, with original crown of thorns and three brass radiants forced on his brows, is said to date from 1696.

A side entrance to the Dominican Church of San Jerónimo at Tlacochahuaya, Oaxaca. The early friars, in need of an adequate local convent, started construction about 1580 but were curbed by order of the viceroy. It was not until the 17th century that the structure was substantially completed.

frescoes of Tlacochahuaya

Like a perpetual spring within the State of Oaxaca, they continue their influence upon the folk-art of a nation.

"Painted Walls of México" by Emily Edwards in part describes San Jerónimo — "the church interior entirely covered with painted decoration conceived and executed as a unit, is integrally a part of the building — expresses the unity and gaity of Baroque design through painting alone, stuccoed design being absent and gold showing only in the frames of panel paintings of altars — in all-over patterns painted in brilliant reds and blues and dull green upon a surface of graded white".

45

Home of Allen and Dorothy Ellis

Inspired, it is said, by the flower-covered, frescoed walls of San Jerónimo on the preceding pages, Jesús Reyes Ferreira has used a similar, ingenuous technique in depicting this colorfully dressed child, looking out from under quilted, gray-blue curtains.

46

Using a more sophisticated subject but similar in its provocative execution, Señor Reyes, known as "Chucho", painted an exotic dancer on plywood, one of several panels which combined to make a tropical-colored, arresting screen.

47

Home of Juan José Torres Landa

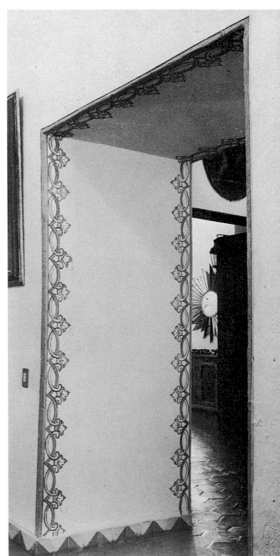

Home of Arturo Alonso

Designs in fresco, used to outline wall openings, recesses and murals of México since the 16th century continue their popularity. *Above:* After three steps up and behind a simple iron balustrade, the study entrance is bordered by a feathery vine-pattern in three colors. *Opposite:* The rounded corners of the opening between entry hall and the long living-dining areas on Page 29 are painted a light wood color. A more robust running design in red and blue outlined in black borders the wide jambs.

Zimapan's parish church, San Juan Bautista, built during the 16th century, has an impressive *Baroque* entrance. A massive pilaster treatment is bordered by frescoed panels in an odd, geometric design; half circles in earth-red removed from earth-red triangles.

The vast ceiling of the Lobby is composed of 8 inch square by 4 inch deep, metal boxes, alternately opened and blanked, all painted an oyster-white. With sufficient frequency to provide adequate lighting, electric bulbs are concealed in the empty boxes.

Hotel El Camino Real

A heavy, moulded-plank door opens on the Gothic
vaulted entrance hall of a very early Puebla home.
Beyond is the inner *patio* on the following page.

Bazar de los Sapos

On the grass plot, a diminutive San Martín gives his cloak to a beggar; rear, is the fountain shown also on a following page. The passageway above, carried on twin arches, shelters a secluded lounging area.

From the passageway over the *patio*, the octagonal lantern by which this house was originally known, *Casa de la Cúpula*, predominates the skyline. A small square lantern topped by a carved-stone jardiniere, is supported on an orange-yellow, tiled dome.

The *patio's* principal feature is this stately wall fountain. All from local gray *cantera*, the top shell, flamelike on its pedestal, gives precedence to the three powerfully carved shells below.

A rope molding in plaster, knotted and tasseled, is a decorative feature over an archway in the *Bazar de los Sapos*, a museum-like antique gallery.

The importance of evil spirits has been traditional. Like the gargoyles of the Middle ages, this *quimera,* a vicious, brass lion, has for many years hurled defiance from the stair newel of his home.

Bazar de los Sapos

The stairways of the early mansions in Palma on the island of Majorca, were protected on their open sides by Gothic, carved and pierced stone rails, similar to those in Barcelona. With the coming of the Renaissance, however, a change occurred which found expression in balustrades of sheet-iron, relatively thin in gauge, instead of the heavier stone. Bold in silhouette, they might well be over-sized prototypes of our turned balusters.

56

This classic building, the national university center since its conversion in 1540, was the former royal palace.

Here, the balustrade rising from the newel in the lower picture opposite, joins another post at the intermediate landing. Similar to the starter with a turned brass finial, it is anchored at the base by an ornate, forged-iron tie-back.

A feature of the façade opposite in Coimbra, Portugal, is the use of flat-iron for balusters. A running succession of cut-outs carry up the several access stairs, between the columns of the first floor gallery and across the open second floor terrace flanking the pedimented, stately arches.

Retrato de la M. R. M. Mª Sor Mª Cayetana Josefa Religiosa Capuchina del Convento de Salto murió el dia 23 de Agosto de 1870 de edad de 54 años, y de religion 31, sirbió varios oficios, y ultimamente la Prelacia por el espacio de doce años. Fué originaria de Guadalajara en el Pueblo de Cocula.

An oil portrait, painted after her death in 1870, of the Reverend Mother, Mª Cayetana Josefa of the Capuchina order; her last twelve years were served as a prioress. She holds a *ramillete* of red roses and one white lily against a palm leaf, while her placid brows are wreathed with reddish *zempasuchitls*, flowers of the marigold family.

58

Beyond old doors, the loggia overlooks a gardened *alberca*. Unusual wood columns whose prototypes are in Pátzcuaro, a heavily beamed ceiling and flagged floor combine with planting and colorful paintings to form an intimate, three-sided living area.

Home of Lena Gordon

A former Colonial residence of notable proportions located a short way up the twisting mountain road which runs past the old Post House on Page 102 is now the Parador San Javier. In the restoration and enlargement, its earlier atmosphere has been carefully preserved. The *cancela* below, between the reception hall and dining room, although not unique is unusual because all of its turned spindles are vertical.

A part of the tap room with its off-white walls and heavily beamed ceiling has a chimney-shelf filled with glazed mugs, copper plates and copper pitchers of all descriptions. The fluted breast recalls the *brasero* hoods in many old-time Mexican kitchens.

Right: Painted by self-taught Miguel Piñeda, two sagacious owls on an enameled tray 10½ inches square, regard the midnight scene.

Mezzanine Shop

Late 17th century Indian conception of the Crucifixion. Under the initial letters of Jesus Nazarenus Rex Judaeorum, a deathly white Cristo, with black hair flowing from under a gilded metal crown of the *potencía*, is spiked to a dull green cross.

With an overall height of 44 inches and a spread of 17 inches, the interior of the open-faced box is painted in earth colors, now faded, oranges and reds. Above the cross, the Heavenly Father looks down on his Son, while immediately below, a representation of the Moon on the left side faces the Sun on the right. Floral designs over the balance of the surfaces, except at the foot of the cross where the flames of Hell form a background consuming three agonized souls and two separate clay skulls.

Draped over the arms of the Cross is a swag of lace. This same lace is repeated as the top and bottom ruching of Christ's short, red silk, quilted skirt, decorated with golden balls. The figure is movingly and realistically carved with great delicacy: another instance of early Mexican artistry.

Home of Humberto Arellano Garza

In a white-walled bedroom a portrait in red and white with dark green background hangs on the tobacco-brown chimney breast. Below is Matilde Poulat's first water pitcher, formed in copper with silver adornments. Cast plaster in squares of brown on white dramatize the ceiling.

63

Here and opposite are choice groupings of furniture assembled from Mexican sources.

In a gorgeous frame of gold-leafed, carved wood, a painting, somewhat obscure, of the Annunciation hangs above the cabriole-legged writing table of pine beside an old treasured *estípite*.

Opposite: Looking through and over the cresting of a Victorian settee, the commode with curved ends is placed under an exquisite painting of the Virgin Mary. She stands on an inverted crescent out of which look six tiny, winged angels. Her finely modeled face under a golden crown contrasts with a background of deep cardinal-red curtains outlined by embossed gold cutouts. Although the general color of the painting is moss-green, her overcape is in "Mary-blue" with dimly picked-out patterns of gold.

Home of Ray Coté

Henry Wynkoop's sala: for curtains and upholstery, Louis XIII cotton print in blues and greens on white, cheered by bright red poppies — made in México by Christian Fersen.

Outside the preceding *sala*, a refreshing loggia overlooks Taxco's roofs and its frequent fiestas.

Except for the papier-mâché "Judas" on the left, quite surely destined to be burned during a Holy Week, the other figures are anxious to be parts of coming gay celebrations. *Above:* Hodas por Fiestas, a group of characters appropriately painted on paper-covered armatures vary from a carnival glass-blower to a dashing *caballero* waiting to be decorated with his firecrackers. *Opposite:* Olga Costa de Chávez-Morado emphasizes the height of figures in the *Alhóndiga de Granaditas* museum. Carried on men's shoulders, they may prance along a narrow Guanajuato street during the next fiesta.

A shocking dragon of the México City family who traditionally create *alabrijas*. Standing 66 inches high, its entire body is painted with red-accented tear-drops in shrieking yellow on a luminous green and blue background. A badly gored hunter is about to be crushed in the beast's orange and fern-green jowls, while his companion has embedded a spear in the creature's neck. Evil predominates!

topmost
backrail

0   1   2   3   4 inches

middle rail

70

Villa Montaña

Gouge-carving in 17th century Spain was frequently employed to ornament various flat surfaces. Brought to México, this method of decoration was widely used by the Tarascans of the Lake Pátzcuaro region on chairs and many other objects of daily use. This old and rugged pine piece, detailed opposite, exemplifies their craftsmanship.

Three traditional seats, two with tasseled cushions of velvet, assembled without nails and the third, a *taburete* with cowhide seat. Below, a Silla Reina, or Queen's chair, a type used for seating the accused while questioned by the Inquisition.

Easily dismountable for hand transportation, the low wood chair is known as a "Shepherd's chair".

With straps to hold a throw of unsheared lambskin, the *taburete* incorporates the graceful curves of a *butaca*.

Bazar de los Sapos

Sala de Artes

72

Home of Pedro M. Peon de Regil

In the hall of this Mérida home leading to a wide, shaded loggia, chairs are grouped for a causerie. That on the right with its flowing lines and shaped legs is a classic *butaca*, so popular in México. Drawings in early manuscripts show chairs with similar leg construction used in 16th century New Spain.

Home of Theodore Dreier

Above, a Mexican adaptation of the English open splat translated in simpler construction. Its lack of ornamentation is compensated by the pleasingly rhythmic outlines of the horizontal back members and apron.

Its colors now muted by age, the 65 inch bench below was a gay piece, with its scalloped back, rippled apron and stretchers. On a sienna background an ubiquitous, double-headed eagle is between two exotic birds, and a medley of greenish-whites, olive-greens and pinkish-sienna flowers.

Home of Dorothy Macdonald

One of the several Chiapas-like benches providing occasional rest in the halls of El Camino Real, México City, with gouged decoration on the vertical and long horizontal, shaped members.

Across the backrail is incised a quaint parade of motifs. Two silly hunters with guns pointed at a favored, double-headed eagle are protected by flower motifs from the pursuing animals.

75

On a parallel wall and around the corner from that below, this lantern with its dancing supports adds spice to the austerity of the main entrance.

Designed by its owner, the rough, rubble masonry wall of the two-story library wing over the entrance court, contrasts sharply with the simplicity of its coping, window surround and adjoining wall. The iron *reja* is from the State of Chiapas. Its finely formed, vertical members carry a scrolled cresting quite similar to some in Oaxaca.

a

younger

Puebla

home

*Home of Marco
and Helga Barocio*

In preparing for construction, the Barocios had gathered some rare pieces, many from the *Bazar de los Sapos,* to incorporate in their future home. Over the inviting, red-cushioned pew in the foyer, a railed stair leads to the library. Pierced, wood motifs from a former altar, here applied on panels, substitute for balusters.

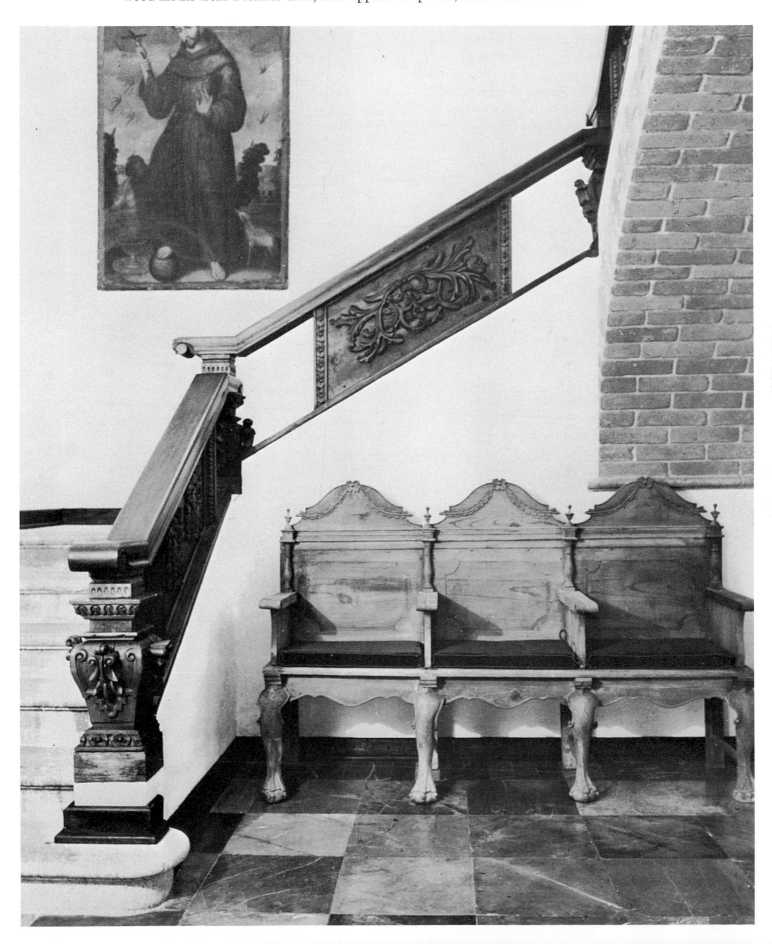

From the preceding stair hall, beyond a pair of old doors from San Miguel de Allende, a white-walled passage leads to the *sala*, where above the arched opening, two angels hold a welcoming stone plaque *"Ésta es su Casa"*. Under the high vaulted ceiling of natural pinkish brick, three typical processional lanterns are hung in an unusual, but decorative fashion — upside-down.

This splendidly framed picture over a handsome carved chest on the left of the passage above, was cleaned a few years ago. It was then that the dingy, old painting, signed by a 17th century Italian artist, revealed this delightful portrait of Mary and the infant Jesus, each with a gilded crown of silver.

The stalwart character of the *comedor's* cross brick vaulting as viewed from the
lower *sala:* Flemish type chandelier, leather upholstered chairs, and Dutch dresser
at right are offset by the delicately crocheted table cover, a carved and gilded
former minor altar at left, and the soft, velvet, olive-green carpeting.

Diagonally opposite the stair landing below is a writing table of colonial Mexican design. Aprons carved in low relief, conventionalized *pájaros* for legs, and stretchers are ornamented on both faces by an interlocking guilloche.

In the white walls of the study are six single and one double wood lined cases for books and memorabilia. The crestings are similar. They recall the more extravagantly broken pediment of a Chippendale china cabinet, silhouetted below, in Puebla's famous *Casa de Alfeñique*.

Home of Marco and Helga Barocio

A shaded, stone-columned loggia of ample width, faces the paved *patio* and its *cantera* fountainhead and basin. With the window openings on three sides protected by old, iron *rejas* from Puebla and Oaxaca, the fourth side is an arcade, partially smothered by bouganvillea.

Standing guard at the terrace above, one of the two heavily maned stone lions laughs with any friendly visitor.

Irregular, oatmeal colored tile, some plain, some decorated with a lacy pattern of dark blue, add distinction as well as utilitarian advantages to this cooking area. The design incorporates features of the *brasero* in the tiled Colonial kitchen of Santa Rosa, a local convent.

A sedimentary, light brown rock, "Xalnene", found in Valsequillo near Puebla, has little value as a structural material. Mowever, when laid up with deeply raked joints, it becomes an unusual, textured garden wall.

Detail of sliding steel entrance door to Casa de las Artesanias de Jalisco: faced with 7½ inch by 14¾ inch tiles, painted by Jorge Wilmot, Salvador Vásquez and Gilberto Pila in the "Tonalá" manner on white backgrounds in tones of blues with bronze touches in stems and animal faces.

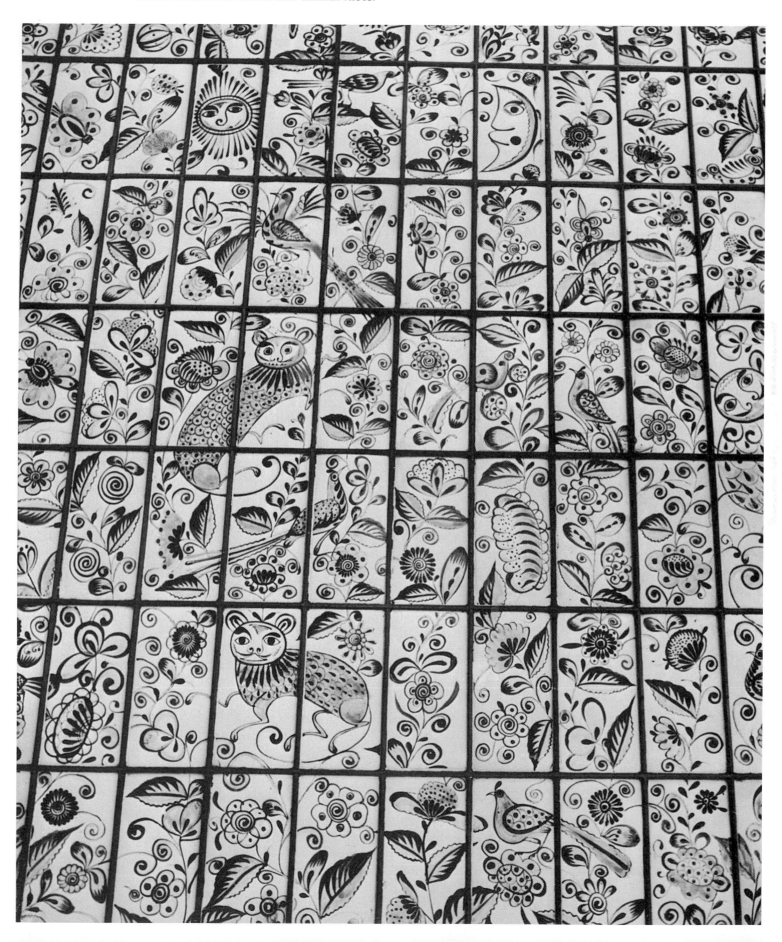

Home of Humberto Arellano Garza

A *cabaña* in Spanish is a cabin or small house, whereas a *cabana* is a bath house.
Above is part of one side of the entrance to an unusual and well appointed *cabaña*,
hidden among the high trees south of Monterrey.

The working area of this *cabaña:* mellowed brick with white and blue tile inserts; multiple *braseros* in the foreground; a sink under the barred opening; twin, tile-framed grilles for barbecues, and a domed oven big enough to roast a goat.

Across a sun drenched, sea-green pool, framed with pink *cantera* flagging and watched-over by a gray *cantera* poodle, is the *cabana* above. Delicately frescoed arches separate the upper from the lower level. Over the fireplace of salmon colored tiles stands an impressive carved stone plaque in high relief of the Virgen de Guadalupe.

Home of Humberto Arellano Garza

Maybe it is the magic of the curved fire-box tapering upward in tepee-fashion or the grouping of scissor-chairs around a former brazier now filled with paper flowers under a glass cover which casts the happy spell over this casual pool house.

While opposite, lead snails of French origin, slither across the coping of Francisco García's garden pool.

Cast in bronze, using the lost wax process, Dorothy Whitehouse sculptured this appealing figure of Saint Francis, now standing in a sylvan alcove near the garden pool below. Legend has it that the walled, hill-town of Gubbio, not far from Assisi, was molested by a vicious wolf. He attacked the people and carried off their children. Terrified, the elders asked Francis, then noted for his love of and power over wild beasts, to help. In 1267 A.D., a meeting at the town gate included elders, the wolf and Saint Francis. The wolf gave Francis his paw in apology for his past misdemeanors and a pact was drawn. In return for protection, the wolf renounced his former ways. As years passed, he became the town's symbol, now used as a design on much of its ceramics.

Below: A shallow, sun-lit pool filled with white blooming plants, is watched over by two chubby water-babies carved from gray *cantera.*

Home of Pedro Chapa

Home of Theodore Dreier

With an old water-tower on the left, parts of the original aqueduct in the background, La Alfarería de Antigua de San Luisito now has an *alberca*. Bordered by cypress and 100 feet long, it is cut into the sharply rising hillside on the right. A round kiln, used for years by a colony of Guanajuato potters, well known for its product, is today the pool's heater room.

Home of Henry and Freda Moser

Because of its temperate climate, many Cuernavaca homes are graced with *albercas* enjoyed throughout the year. From this arched loggia, actually a three-sided outdoor living room, a heavily vined, double archway terminates in *obeliscos*.

Opposite is a detail, not carved from stone but elaborately ornamented with the cement scroll-work of a *maestro*.

92

A portion of the restored scalloped wall which partially encloses the wooded garden of Museo del Virreinato. The *museo* was originally a part of the 16th century convent and magnificent Jesuit church in Tepotzotlán. Dark brown *cantera* piers, exposed between rubble walls are topped by squared mouldings supporting turned urns in light-gray *cantera*.

93

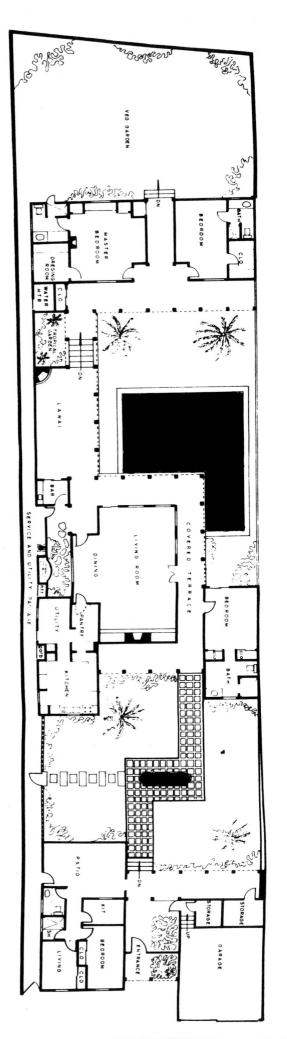

simplicity, grace
and 39 arches

Home of the Horace Carletons

Several steps within the street entrance lead to an arcade overlooking the patio on this and on the preceding page; a small pool surrounded by a cheerfully informal flower and fruit garden. Lanterns with concealed bulbs shining through golden amber and dusty gray-green translucent globes light the bordering arched ways. To the left is that handsome French gate on Page 25. Distinctive to the plan of this unique house is complete privacy obtained by separating rooms with corridors. Honors go to Florence Noyes Carleton, architect and co-owner.

A deep shaded lanai with its corner fireplace for the occasional cool evening is separated from the *alberca* by four pillars covered with purple flowering bean vines; a favorite feeding place for innumerable humming birds.

Under an intense blue sky and billowing clouds over Cuernavaca, the chaste arches of a very unusual home are reflected in its "L" shaped swimming pool.

Exciting in outline against the sky a white stuccoed wall with decorations in low relief, painted in familiar Portuguese "Mary Blue", the façade of empty pasture land. It adjoins the parish house behind an octagonal church on the road from Óbidos to Nazaré, Portugal.

Apparently this charming realization of some designer's skill had three purposes: to record for posterity the gentleman who stands just underneath the moulded crest holding an open scroll, to form the background of the circular water basin at its foot, and to leave in the mind of the passer a remembrance of beauty.

A façade in San Fernando on·the Cádiz highway, exceptional for its studied and dignified simplicity. An imaginative over-door treatment carries in addition to its elongated central finial, an added broken pediment which effects a rich composition. Moulded window canopies and the delicate urns on parapet wall above combine to produce a minor masterpiece.

In contrast with the spirited façade above, that opposite is unusual in its reticence and elegance of line and detail. Although their structures are iron, these exquisite Córdova balconies might well have been the dream of a skilled jeweler.

100

la cochera de la Valenciana

Originally, the building above was used by the Marqués de San Clemente and from which he operated his Cata and the famous Mellado silver mines. Later, it became a Post House on the Guanajuato-Dolores road over the Sirena mountains. The front, substantially unchanged through several centuries, is of warm gray stucco over rubble masonry with openings trimmed in local, greenish-gray stone. The similarity between the over-window treatment of this construction, high in the hills above Guanajuato, and that of an old convent opposite, in the valley of Oaxaca, is very interesting.

Home of John and Emily Haugh

The preceding entrance door opens into a white walled *zaguán*. A native flagstone floor is subdivided by herringbone brick panels. Past an old bench of wide mesquite boards below a processional lantern, the calm wrought iron *cancela* from a former Oaxaca home gives access to the open *patio* on following page.

103

Because of the great number of *ranas* which lived on the surrounding slopes, the original Tarascan name for Guanajuato was Guanaxhuato, mening "Hill of Frogs". Beyond the arched opening a covered terrace provides commanding views of these hills, with old mine buildings in the background. The *patio* with its rough masonry and off-white stuccoed walls is ideal for protected sunning.

Under its flooring of greenish and rose flagstone is an extensive rain-water cistern. Its opening, on the preceding page, protected by the moulded, *cantera* curbing, has a wrought iron pulley standard decorated with delicate volutes. An afternoon sun casts the sharp shadow of a 32 inch high processional lantern. Simple in design, painted a Venetian red, the cross within a full radiance forms a novel cresting.

In the *sala* of the Haugh home an unconventional cabinet rests on a low cupboard. Below a domed head and shaped frieze, delicate pilasters and pierced guilloche wings are gilded, brightening the stained *sabino*. Originally, glass replaced the front and side panels. Then the cabinet housed a locally venerated saint when, on an *anda*, he was carried in religious processions.

Home of John and Emily Haugh

Intricately made, this two-headed eagle on a lantern was assembled by a *maestro*.
Formed with bits of translucent glass held by lead cames, the lordly bird overlooks
the stair of the Parador Nacional Condestable Davalos, Ubeda, Spain.

Home of Joseph and Viola Turner

Above, one of a pair of lanterns flanking a library entrance. Mounted on carved *cantera* bases, elliptical cages of pierced metal are topped by crowns and flaming suns.

Forged iron "S" scrolls, decorated with rosettes, culminate in a small cross and form the bracket for a lacy lantern in the refurbished Alcázar of Seville.

Left, modern conceptions of the processional lantern with ebonized poles light the *corredores* of the *Casa del Balam*. Green glass over amber borders tops the leaded cage whose central motif is the outline of a conventionalized monstrance in green glass.

Home of Francisco García Valencia

Replicas of the centuries-old processional lantern are clustered together on their carrying poles as garden torches, or their variously pierced hoods may cast glimmers of light when mounted between wrought iron bracket-arms or perched upon fanciful scroll.

A brass chandelier hangs from the high ceiling of the former chapel of an old convent, now Parador Nacional de Mérida. From its vase-like baluster stem, three tiers of delicately pierced arms carry the illumination.

The wall lanterns opposite, designed by Gene Byron, are of tin, brass and copper. That above, with a cresting of pierced copper and brass strips, happens to hold two small figures from Oaxaca. Below, the glass sides of a 22 inch high lantern are decorated with tooled and pierced lozenge motifs.

The vase-shaped lamps throw light both downward and sideways with the source concealed in the throat, while from the globe, light shines through all the varied openings in its surface.

A recent and delightfully refreshing style of incidental lighting found in Sala de Artes. These pierced ceramic pieces with gray and black designs on glazed white backgrounds cast fanciful shadows.

The entrance foyer of Seville's *Alcázar* presents ironwork with reborn zest and elegance in style. Over a paving, alternating squares of miniature pebbles and marble, and flanked by white marble engaged columns, rises this veil-like tracery of an iron gate.

Between white stuccoed walls ending in gray *cantera* piers, these charming iron gates protect the entrance driveway of a Cuernavaca home. The basic design in swirls and fleur-de-lis is interwoven with grape-like tendrils terminating in embossed, stylized leaves.

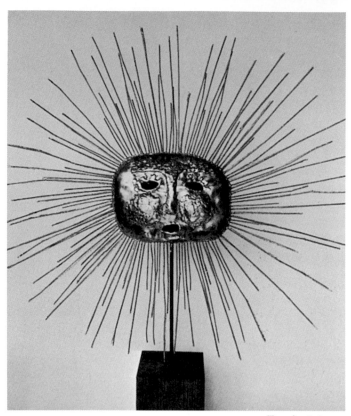

The unusual metal design above and that on the following page are the results of a young man's imagination, Angel Ocampo. Working with associates, schooled in the use of the torch, these oddities are fabricated on the grounds of the former Benedictine monastery mentioned on Page 12.

The puffing sun radiates spectacular beams. The fish opposite, with its green and red glass eyes, has fins of dark bronze. Otherwise, these hollow creations have a golden luster.

Museo de la Cerámica

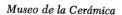

Parador de Nerja, Malaga, Spain

This pottery ship in outrageous colors, enlivened with *mariachis* and dancers, must have been some person's hallucination, after an evening on Lake Chapala.

8 x 8 inch white tiles, many decorated with stylized rosettes, wheels in blues and deep greens, and the twin white fireplace hoods completely occupy one wall of a lounge in the Parador de Nerja overlooking the Mediterranean near Malaga, Spain.

Becomingness of home to owners usually reflects keen discrimination. Dorothy
and Allen Ellis have transplanted their high-keyed northern coloring, their tastes
and belongings into an indoor-outdoor home befitting of their fancy on the border

of Cuernavaca. Indelible views are framed by two bays. An intimate composition centers around Guadalupe, seen over an old chest handsomely brass-studded. Below, a balustraded terrace appears to extend this bay; an all white bed room, catching here and there the green of the palms.

A weighing machine of ancient lineage: released now from its everyday usage, this tall, brass scale on a carved and gilded wood base has its dishes filled with colorful wax fruits and white daisies under a portrait by Caroline Durieux.

Home of Allen and Dorothy Ellis

With and later following the *Conquistadores* came master craftsmen to New Spain, many from Andalucia. Zealous to maintain the quality of their skills, an ordinance was confirmed in 1568 establishing the classifications of an apprentice, journeyman and *maestro.* In addition, it described their required skills including those of carpenters, joiners, lutemakers, carvers and others. To be recognized as a carver, it was necessary for the artisan to be also adept in marquetry. Described by Carlos de Ovando in *Artes de México*, marquetry is "the decorative inlay work of small pieces of natural or dyed woods, ivory, bone, mother-of-pearl, tortoiseshell and other materials".

On a substitute stand, an earlier *vargueño* is a handsome example of marquetry. The drawers and shelf of the interior with their contrasting inlay in geometric designs are typical of the Moorish tradition. On the drop front delicately executed in etched ivory, vines branch out from a coat of arms surrounded by four doves. Alfonso on the left offers his heart to Alena who reaches to accept it: undoubtedly a wedding gift of the 1700's.

Above is an exquisite example of tortoise-shell combs so highly prized. This delicately pierced work-of-art, ranging from dark to light amber in color, is 13½ inches wide.

Señora Carmen Pérez de Salazar de Ovando wears another of her ancestral combs to show that, when properly placed under a *mantilla* of old Spanish lace, a picture of rare distinction results.

The interior of the upper cabinet, 24 inches wide, is painted an orange-tinted Mexican pink and filled with shallow drawers and four small cupboards. Decorated with floral designs in pale blue, pinky-red, soft olive and yellow-green leaves, the top is outlined in gold leaf. Similarly outlined on the door interiors are ovals enclosing miniatures of a man and woman, quite likely the couple for whom this spirited desk was crafted.

Created by a Puebla master craftsman, this mudéjar-style writing desk is in two parts. Inset with bone and native woods, the wood marquetry on the ends and front is flush, while the etched bone marquetry on the front is both flush and pillowed.

Home of Carlos de Ovando

Below, calm simplicity is the keynote of the high ceilinged *sala* of the Orepesa *Parador* and its crowned lanterns.

Shaded entrance drive to Dolores Noriatenco, a former *hacienda* now within Puebla's city limits.

Heavy wood doors protected the entry passage leading to the inner yard on the following page, past the *hacendado*'s office adjoining a vast *bodega*, now little used.

Home of Ing. Miguel Díaz Barriga

A view from the "U" shaped loggia of the main house looking toward the box stalls of an extensive stable bounding the far side of the yard. Young Mr. Barriga is up on one of his father's polo ponies.

A gracious *sala* with many rare and treasured objects. Beyond the center arch hangs a handsome, crystal chandelier, while narrowly spaced oak beams supporting the 23 foot high ceiling give an illusion of corduroy which dominates the room.

Used foils and dueling swords decorate a library wall above an intricately carved Italian chair.

White plastered walls over a dado of red brick with tile inserts, typical of Puebla, surround a loggia floored with semi-rough, multi-colored Santo Tomás marble. A crucified Christ on a carved and heavily gold-leafed cross with mirror inlays hangs

Barriga

Brand

Home of Ing. Miguel Díaz Barriga

in a recess bordered by the rich blue tile inserts of the dado. In a corner — opposite, Santiago on his blond stallion is riding down a Moor. Carved from wood, *gessoed* and painted in high key, the grouping is eloquent with action.

127

The new front of an old shop in *Talavera* de la Reina, Spain, now bears the name "Potter of Small Objects". It was from this city that Spanish artisans came to New Spain bringing with them the knowledge and skill of making glazed ceramics inherited from the Moors.

The early Arabic name for tiles, "small burnt stone", was Zulache or Zuleija. Later, when blue or *azul* metallic oxides were used as the predominate design color, they were called *azulejos*, as they are today.

Back of the modern store window, is a small *taller* of indefinite age. Previously decorated bowls, now used as samples, cover an end wall. The balance of the barn-like structure is filled with Talavera ware in all of its various stages of production.

128

Home of Carlos de Ovando

In the later 1860's, Puebla potters took pleasure twitting the previously withdrawn Frenchmen, formerly under Maximilian. Obviously an officer, goatee and mustachio, is here only a jug, 12 inches high.

Used as a baptismal font for many years, the bowl below is an old and rare piece, 20½ inches in diameter and 7 inches deep. With the design in deep blue on white, a colonial gentleman strides through his vineyard.

Bazar de los Sapos

Centro Regional de las Artesanias y el Folklore

An example of *Talavera* ware of the 18th century made in Puebla. The blue floral and bird motifs are repeated above and below around this 23 inch tall jar.

129

Home of Joseph and Viola Turner

Emaús, S.A.—*Sol Cabello Largo*—a metal portrait of a bewildered Sun spinning through a terrifying storm of winds: over-all width 22 inches.

Museo Nacional de Artes e Industrias Populares

Mermaids are highly favored in Mexican decorative schemes. In the guest bath shower, a *sirena* in predominating colors of green and apricot, on a wall of pearly-white Puebla tile, greets you from behind green curtains.

Opposite, an enticing multi-colored *sirena* from Metepec, brightly glazed and flowered with chi-chi of the sea, carries a fish on her head. This pottery extravagancy is, in fact, only a candle holder.

130

Embedded in the circular plaque over the door are two amber-colored codfish oil bottles of the late 19th century in honor of Mr. Arellano's birth sign, Pisces. The surrounding walls of the bath are tiled in the popular half-handkerchief or *medio-pañuelo* pattern of Moorish origin. Here, the two differing methods of arranging the same tile have created an unusual and impressive effect.

Home of Humberto Arellano Garza

Home of Marco and Helga Barocio

A boldly carved and heavily gilded wood mirror frame is a striking feature of another guest bath, which gains added elegance by the use of bright brass fittings and accessories in conjunction with a gray carved stone lavatory.

Below are two tiles from historic Dolores Hidalgo, patterned in two shades of blue on oatmeal white.

131

Bazar de los Sapos

Home of Matilde Holbert

The art of making glazed tiles, introduced to Spain by the Moors, lends bits of color to Mexican homes. The risers of an old stair in Puebla are faced with dark-blue, tight swags while those in a Cuernavaca home, right, are decorated with blue-white festoons, both on off-white grounds. A base tile in San Miguel de Allende, white with a yellowish-pink design topped by a bead of orange-pink is tailored to follow the flagstone treads.

Home of Francisco García Valencia

Home of Henry and Freda Moser

Up a short flight of tile-faced steps, this pebble-paved and luxuriously arbored *túnel* leads from the walled street entrance past a guest suite before arriving at the door on the next page.

A glazed door with halved and shaped flat members, performs the functions of a
cancela as well as protecting the loggia beyond from occasional, unwelcome drafts.

Home of Henry and Freda Moser

Home of Thomas Briscoe Miller

Former Home of Felipe Teixidor

The doors of New Spain varied markedly in design. Some with Moorish geometric patterns of interlacing straight and curved panel arrangements framing ornamental detail from 16th century Italy, a traditional style known as *mudéjar*, as in left above.

Others with simple raised panels rely on cast bosses, both structural and ornamental for their decoration. Opposite, the *postigo* of a pair of doors in Ubeda carries a lion's head with twin goats forming the *llamador*, surrounded by an overabundance of bosses.

"La *Danza*" from the state of Vera Cruz; a pre-Hispanic vivacious pottery dancer of the period when a blackened mouth was considered an allurement. One of the José Chávez-Morado loan collection to the *Alhóndiga de Granaditas*, now a Guanajuato museum.

Home of José and Olga Costa de Chávez-Morado

The approach to the former 17th century Hacienda Santa Guadalupe de Pastita is up a narrow paved road alongside one of Guanajuato's mountain streams and ends under the high arched aqueduct in the background. Placed over a well, the former tank room of this partially reconstructed *torre* supplied water to adjoining hillside sections. Now, the tank room is a high-ceilinged studio, above but adjoining living areas — the home of José Chávez-Morado, and his wife, Olga Costa.

la torre

A gracious *sala* fireplace whose shelf carries and is surrounded by diverse objects representing a meeting of several cultural streams. On the right, "Santa Olga" so-called because the saint who previously occupied this sumptuous pierced and gilded frame, is now replaced by Chávez-Morado's profile of his wife.

From a position opposite the fireplace, the tile floored *sala* ends at the open flights of stone stairs leading to the studio above. The construction of the curved brick ceiling without the use of forms is an attainment unique with a Lago de Moreno family of masons.

139

Home of José and Olga Costa de Chávez-Morado

Crosses of painted wood and stone portraying symbols associated with the Cruci-fixion are frequently seen in México. Here is an especially prized stone cross. Carved by an Otomí Indian after conversion by an early *padre*, it expresses, using some pre-Hispanic ideograms, his understanding of the tragedy. Just above the base, a representation of water, the source of life, is followed by a spike, rooster, a bleeding hand and stars. A resplendant sun, so beloved by all peoples, is the central feature.

Beyond an arch of paper *zempasuchitles*, this chapel-like alcove in the Alhóndiga of Guanajuato is decorated with objects of religious significance assembled by Chávez-Morado. Of principle interest is the sack-cloth gown with red face-mask and braided rope worn by a carrier of an *anda* in Holy Week processions.

141

Under shallow brick arches and several steps down from the studio on the following page, this bedroom is merry because of its many contrasts. Frosty mornings are tempered by a little cast iron stove, a *"Chihuahuense"*, while a dainty, gilded Japanese fan flirts with the honest, free-standing smoke pipe as it angles upward. Above the "Ranchero Victorian" mesquite double bed hangs a silk tapestry from Cambodia.

Opposite, a crown worn by a noviciate at the time of her marriage to the Church. Tiny wax figures in multi-colored rich robes are emphasized by masses of green leaves and red, white and pink cloth flowers.

Home of José and Olga Costa de Chávez-Morado

Off the entrance court on Page 137, the Chávez-Morados are building another but more spacious studio. When completed, this former tank room of the old *torre* becomes the working studio of Olga Costa, whose oils are on the two easels. Señor will then have ample space for his more diverse artistic activities.

A monogram in relief accented with gold is on an off-white wall of the recently restored 18th century, Oaxaca Ex-Convento de los Siete Príncipes, now a school for handicrafts. The ceiling tile, painted white to form a running saw-tooth pattern is carried by stained beams. Using the same treatment, an interesting under-edging is achieved for the wide roofed overhangs encircling a patio.

The cabinet below with its geometric paneled doors is now only one half of its original size. Designed to be part of a wall with access from the adjoining rooms of a former Querétaro home, it was cut through the middle to form two corner pieces, one of which is here in Belloli's *sala*.

Under a delightfully unsophisticated oil painting of a deceased nun is Mr. Belloli's modern interpretation of a "Dante" chair, whose 16th century ancestor of Italian design was later adopted by the Spanish and brought to New Spain.

Home of Giorgio and Louise Belloli

Sala de Artes

Two splendid chairs of Mexican make but each following a differing foreign trend. Based on earlier tradition, that on the left has a 17th century arcaded back with turned spindles. Designed by Sarita, it complements some modern interpretations of Portuguese headboards of that epoch.

A century later, the curvilinear principle seeped into Spain and then to México from England's Queen Anne, 1702-1727. Results were not always so endearing as in this old chair with its graceful arms ending in double curves, its high open splat back, and its generous seat.

A Japanese warlord returns along the great Tokaido Road between Tokyo and Kyoto with his spoils. On a silk screen, the colorful figures are padded and sewn in low relief depicting their most minute details; an unusual and remarkable example of exquisite needlework.

Two elevations of a very comfortable high-backed chair made in México for Accesorios en Decoración. Its subtly curved upper members and Chinese red, reflect a continuing influence of Oriental spice and flavor.

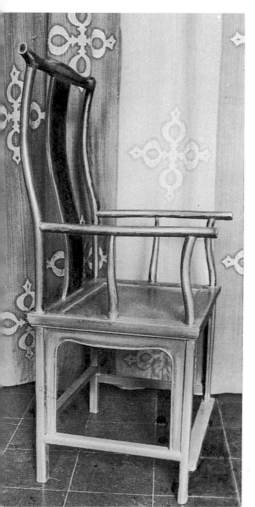

The classic example of a secretary bookcase in mahogany with simple broken pediment, has marked late Chippendale characteristics. The porcelains are in sympathy with the present hardware of Oriental design. A favored "Trinity" motif in low relief on the capitals of the pilasters would suggest this handsome piece to be the work of Mexican craftsmen.

Home of Francisco Cusi

Here and below bits and pieces of old iron hardware: key escutcheons, an "L" strap for a door and a decorative lid hinge.

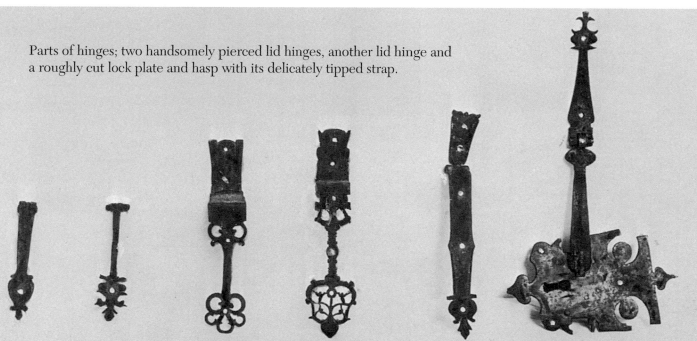

Parts of hinges; two handsomely pierced lid hinges, another lid hinge and a roughly cut lock plate and hasp with its delicately tipped strap.

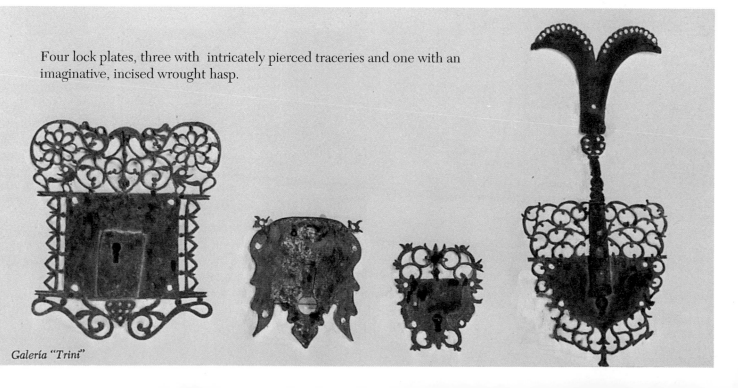

Four lock plates, three with intricately pierced traceries and one with an imaginative, incised wrought hasp.

Galería "Trini"

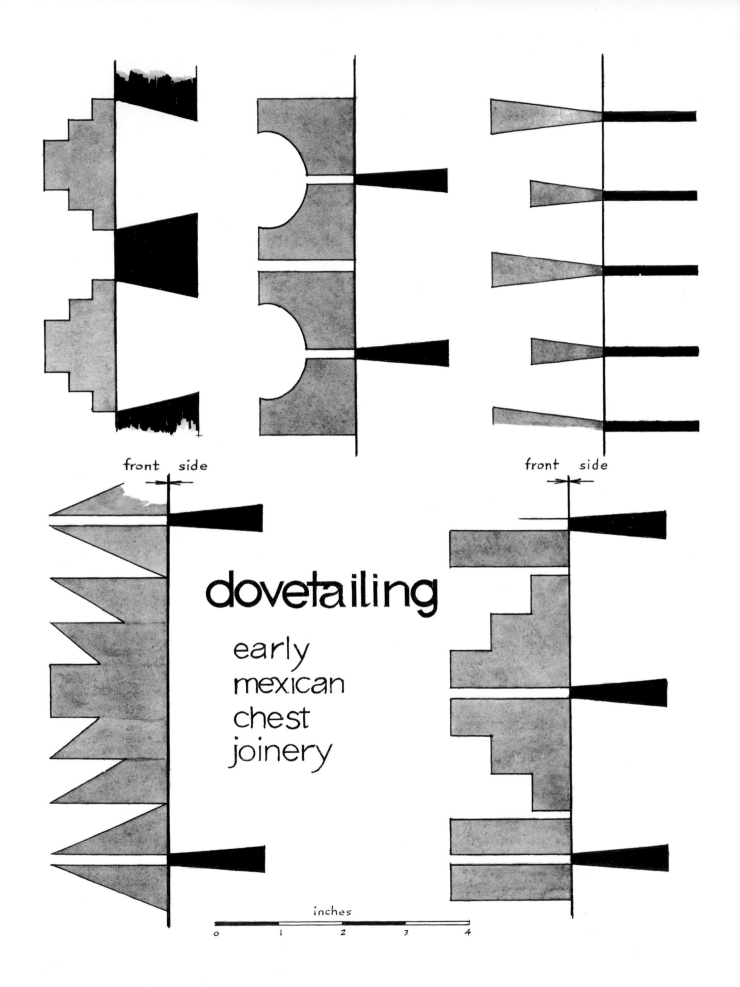

front   side

dovetailing

early
mexican
chest
joinery

front   side

inches

0   1   2   3   4

Of uncertain origin and age, this natural-blond wood chest is magnificently ornamented on its front, ends and lid with a double-interlocking scroll or guilloche. A motif originating with Egyptian decoration and used by the Greeks, here borders naïve panels, all carved by some master craftsman. While the two little birds and scrolls of the center panel are incised, the other front panels are in low relief. The lock plate with a heavy forged iron hasp, is rather crudely pierced.

The lid panels above are carved in deeper relief than those on the front. That on the right with its bewhiskered animal and bird is substantially repeated on the left side of the lid, while in the center panel are two frolicking parrots.

Home of J. B. Johnson

Although papier-mâché pieces are now abundant in many shops, it is exceptional to find a creation of Gemma Tacogna, the artist who popularized her version of this craft in México.

However, here are two, one purchased from and the other harboured by the Mezzanine Shop in México City since 1964. In Henry Wynkoop's Taxco guest house, a brown haired lady with a tight-fitting cap of rusty-green and light green trim becomes a lamp base. Above, adaptable for decorative arrangements, a demure miss, 29½ inches tall, is dressed in warm, antiqued-gray accented by black lozenges. Applied string of the same ground color fashions the shoulder scarf and skirt scrolls.

Home of Arturo Pani and Edward Ballenger

Javier Garza, a local artist, combines his skills in metalwork and painting with his knowledge of floral decoration. Above, a delightfully naturalistic curtain holdback.

On a metal wastebasket 13 inches high, Ann Miller has applied a black-and-white print to a lime-yellow background. Then, accenting the toucan in rich blues with yellow eyes and feet, the whole is cleverly antiqued.

Mezzanine Shop

On an Arturo Pani changeable, blue-green material covering the sofa's end-table, the turned and ribbed wood lamp-standard may have been a luxurious stair baluster. More probably, however, it is the pleasing combination of two identical-twin urns.

153

Museo Nacional de Artes e Industrias Populares

Myths and legends are still prevalent with the Indian peoples of México. Above is a *Nahual*, a being who, according to Aztec legends, would transform itself into an animal when bent on doing some mischief. Jorge Wilmot, the noted potter of Tonalá, has painted on varnished cheesecloth an imaginary *Nahual* who, during the full moon, has become a "City Cat". Blending with the shadowy façades and vague terraces, its tail circles the right while his front paws rest on the twin arcades to the left; an unquestionable aristocrat.

Another creation of Jorge Wilmot: on a typical Huichol *taburete* this obviously knowing ceramic cat is embellished with white daisies and halved seed pods on an unglazed, green background.

154

Tonal decorative values of Japanese design show their impression on this versatile artist. A geometrically arranged school of fish, all blue and greens with very delicate white spots and pencilled outline, typify his meticulous draftsmanship.

155

One of the homes on the walled eminence above the small fishing harbor of Ericeíra, Portugal. Under a frieze painted Indian red, the charm of the buoyant blue tile, over-door design is emphasized by its white stucco background.

This invitingly deep loggia, part of a former *hacendado's* home, now the Hotel Hacienda Chichén, lies among the strikingly picturesque ruins of *Chichén Itzá*. Arches carried on delicate columns form an arcade of great serenity.

From Patric's Arts and Crafts Shop in Mérida come these panels painted on various materials by Patric. On the right, the design is adapted from clay seals while on the left, birds used in Aztec, Toltec cultures are reproduced.

Carápan   *Home of David M. and Anne Wilson*

A raised loggia of the guest house overlooks a paved terrace and the lawn beyond. Constructed of black volcanic rock without coping, the scalloped garden wall is covered with pink and scarlet blooms of climbing geranium. On either side and above the two-tiered fountain, plumed and winged angels carved from pink *cantera* provide the music while four gray *cantera* snarling lions support the table in the foreground.

Displaying his luxuriant plummage, a white plaster peacock from Metepec, 24 inches wide, is a triple candle holder.

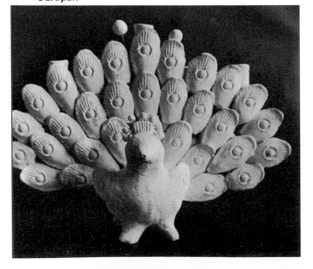

Home of Samuel Chavolla

Built in 1789, the roughly parged rubble masonry wall of this Apaseo el Grande farmyard is in sharp contrast with the fanciful fluting and rounded arch-mould terminating in tight scrolls on the decorated capitals of the pilasters.

Façade of the right half of the double church of Santo Domingo, La Portada de la Capilla del Rosario, Querétaro, with carvings in deep buff *cantera* was completed in 1760. Trent B. Sanford states in *Story of Architecture in México* it is . . .

"—a barbarically naïve interpretation of the *Churrigueresque* with urns in baskets, shell forms, and acanthus-skirted figures with scrolls for shoulders and great plumes for a headdress, showing to what lengths the wild extravagances of that style could be taken".

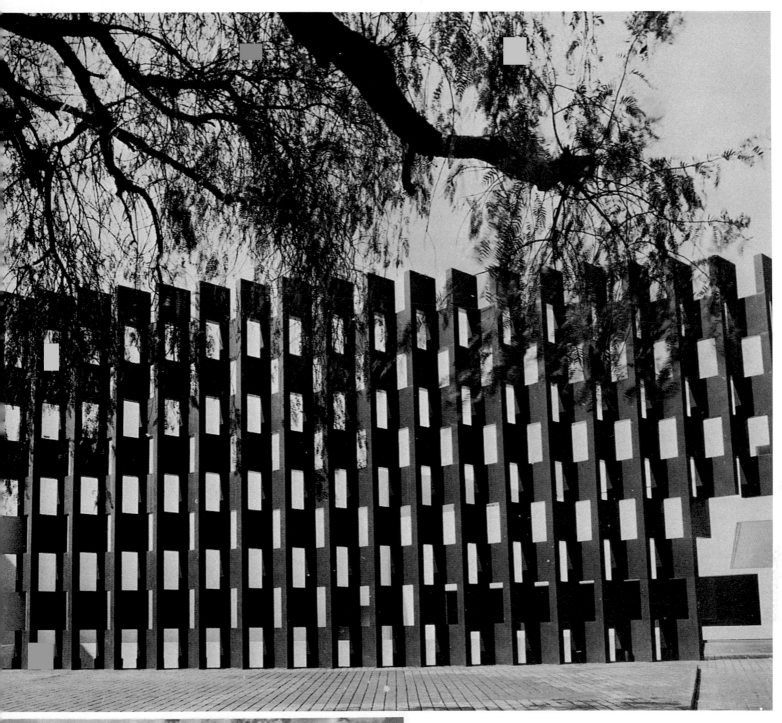

Dramatizing the vehicle entrance of El Camino Real in México City is a novel wall, the work of a noted sculptor, Mathias Goeritz. A series of hollow, abutting metal boxes, 7¾ inches deep rise 30 feet high and present an ever-changing screen to the passer-by. Below, the reverse side becomes a backdrop for a spectacular, marble-lined pool. A bit of ocean is seemingly whirled savagely about by some mysterious monster in its efforts to escape.

161

Slightly crumpled, a thin metal sheet is punctured by varying sized nails from the reverse side, then, brightly gilded to achieve its purpose of reflecting light. One of several 27 inch square panels exhibited by Mathias Goeritz, using a similar technique, differing only in patterning — unique and spellbinding.

162

On the highway from Mérida to *Chichén-Itzá*, an intriguing portal leads to *Hacienda* San Pedro. Built of rubble stone and stuccoed, the vigorous Moorish curves are still cleanly outlined in white, contrasting with the rich Mexican pink now weathered from light shades to deep, brickish red.

Hotel Jurica Querétaro

With few additions but extensive changes, a former *hacendado's* residence has now become a dignified and handsome inn, Hotel Jurica Querétaro. Surrounded by spacious lawns, its old chapel on the left, the reception drive is on the far end of this impressive main façade. Built on pre-Hispanic Tarascan lands just north of Querétaro, the early meaning of the word *"Jurica"* was "Place of Witch Doctor".

A pottery ash tray designed by *Lic.* Humberto Guevara, a Guanajuato lawyer and occasional artist, has been the most popular souvenir with H J Q visitors.

Seen from under rubble stone arches of the paved reception court, a low aqueduct carried water from the *hacienda's* well to the almost level fields beyond.

In pink and gray *cantera*, girdled by the zodiac, a sun-like medallion rides above pink *cantera* floral artistry. Executed under the supervision of José Chávez-Morado, his imaginative and majestically scaled designs add great stature to Hotel Jurica Querétaro.

166

When H J Q was a working *hacienda*, access to the grain storage areas was through this arcade. It continues to form a part of the main façade: a loggia of dignified proportions with ornamented end walls.

In the background, the stone arcade of the former coach house is in sharp contrast with the white stuccoed additions. From its loggia, served by an old style *cantina*, "La Paloma Azul", the view is toward the open courts at the rear of the main building and across the large serpentine *alberca*. The pink *cantera* walk-way complements the green of the lawn, both seemingly intensified by the blue of the water.

Hotel Jurica Querétaro

One end of a lengthy *sala* is closed with squares of blue cathedral glass overlapped by pointed and moulded pieces of stained wood, forming a mystic screening of unusual pattern. Above a long conference table, this impressive fixture, 6 feet in diameter, is hung by chains from a central brass ball just below a delicate, heart-shaped, leafed and budding motif, braced by an eight point brass star.

Upon entering the chapel, an arresting screen in dull red carries, on a delicately scrolled console, an Infant Jesus before a golden radiance, adjoining a *Baroque* plaque, "H J Q". Behind the shield, is the dining room where Indian-red pilasters repeat the exterior buttresses. The cross, over 30 feet high in pink *cantera* and black lava rock, designed by Chávez-Morado, is symbolic of man's growth, blossoming and death.

The bedroom of a handsomely decorated suite reserved for dignitaries. Above the bed-head and under a timbered ceiling, hangs this wondrous, vibrant cross, carved in the Philippines.

Below, the velvet head-board between two built-in shelves repeats the color of the royal-blue wall-to-wall carpeting. A magnificent crocheted white bedspread flows over its elegant background.

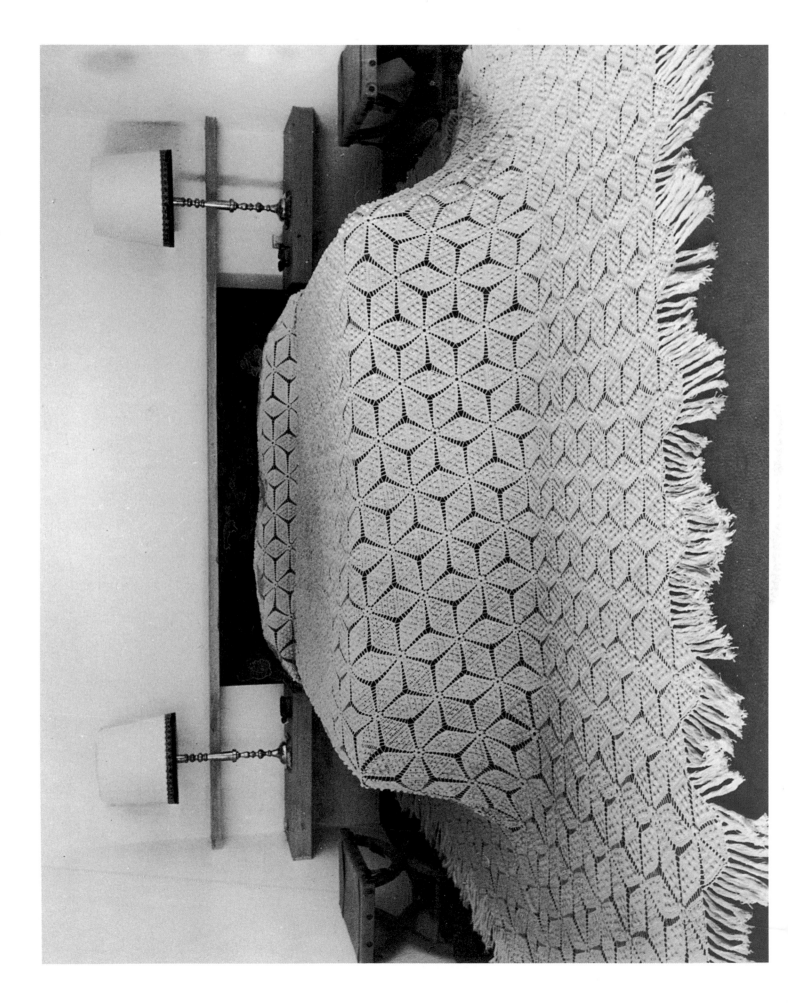

In México where the ground floor is known as "el *piso bajo*", the sundeck below is several steps above the 1st floor. Open to the sky, bordered by the severely plain rear wall of the *sala* on Page 170 and a parapet carrying potted geraniums, it is an ideal land-locked island for relaxation.

Hotel Jurica Querétaro

The deck opposite overlooks the "Patio de Rodas" (Rhodes) whose tree design in obsidian, outlined by white marble spawls, wanders around the rosette motifs of the fountains. This spacious carpeting of pebbles is surrounded by a geometric pattern in blacks and tans between bands of white and black.

The inner garden walks of the *Museo Provincial de Bellas Artes* in Córdoba are paved with black and white pebbles. The capricious designs are varied; "S" scrolls, "C" scrolls, guilloches, vase and other motifs are intermingled between brick borders. When joined by the greenery and occasional statuary, the general effect is one of 19th century romance.

"The Moor was adept at formal gardening and used this art to its fullest extent as a contribution to the enjoyment of life."

Elements of Interior Design and Decoration by Sherrill Whiton

175

Flagstones, river pebbles and white marble chips combine to form an interesting pavement for the entrance court. The flagging and chips are laid with full joints, while the pebbles only slightly bedded, give added texture for the composition.

The ocean front of Figuerira da Foz is a magnificent beach. Paralleling its esplanade, the easterly sidewalk of white marble cubes is broken with black panels, appropriately inset with conventionalized sea creatures.

Striking 36 inch white and black squares of pebbles with occasional courses of red brick pave the terrace overlooking the Mediterranean of the Parador de Nerja, near Málaga.

Home of Henry and Freda Moser

From *alberca* to bath, although only a short distance, the customary flag stepping-stone walk seemed too commonplace for its environment. A series of incised and shaped pieces of pink *cantera* were substituted. Butterflies, leaves and fish, bedded in the grass, make for an amusing journey.

178

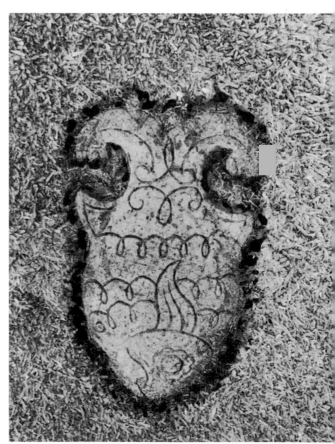

Home of Pedro M. Peon de Regil

An inviting entry: limestone steps to a cool breezeway between the entrance hall and dining area of this Mérida home. Beyond, a loggia overlooks the gardens through the low arches of an arcade.

Photograph by Roy Gordon Werner-Robel   *Home of Oliver and Dorcas Snyder*

A quiet and sunny patio corner in San Miguel de Allende, Galería Villa Roma. Orchids on an orange tree, and a Guerrero jar are the foreground of the abstract acrylic painting, 52 inches high, signed "Oliver".

An intimate, sun-dappled patio, entered under a fern-lined arch. Empire style iron armchairs with white seat pads join the gingham-like tiled wall fountain in creating a cool, crisp feeling.

Home of Frances Stoddard

Casita of Arturo Alonso

Charmingly simple wrought-iron, glazed doors under a fanlight of quaint design, open upon a loggia with its barreled ceiling of red hexagonal clay tile over a semi-rough Puebla marble floor.

A pair of iron gates leading to the *Alcázar* of Córdoba have square vertical members ornamented with six cut-out inserts; the central four are those below.

Taunted by a red *muleta*, this savage bull is poised to charge. Metal sculptures by Manuel Felquérez, a Mexican artist who adds a fresh and novel viewpoint.

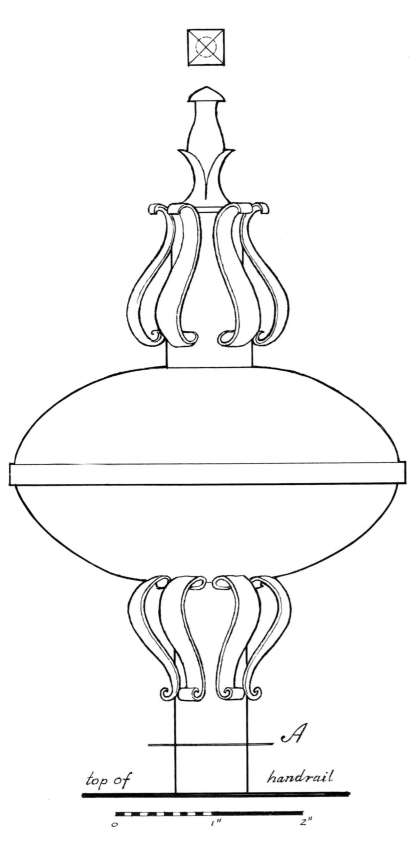

top of   handrail

0   1"   2"

A

Section A
looking up

A wrap-around balcony in Oaxaca has varied iron balusters supporting its assembled sheet-iron railing, braced at the outer corner by flying scrolled bars holding a delicately wrought lily with returns accented by proud finials as shown and detailed.

In *Casa de las Artesanais de Jalisco* a mirror, approximately 12 by 20 inches, is surrounded with a fanciful composition of leaves and rosettes, and held by an incised tin border.

In Botin's famous Toledo restaurant is a magnificent example of pierced tin repoussé. Headed with an anthemion, it is a mass of "S" and "C" scrolls intermixed with leaves and flowers, all done with great delicacy.

Below and opposite, this hallway is a veritable treasure-trove. Inserts of white daisies on blue, highlight the tile flooring. A richly stained dropped ceiling of mitered lattice is carried on transverse beams with carved leaf consoles. Small lowering in height allows electric tubes to give a soft and uniform illumination.

Home of J. B. Johnson

miniature

The various and varied objects of note on these white walls have been gradually acquired. The intricate, sparkling frame above the console is from Peru. At its right, twin portraits, "Le Roy de France — Henry II" and "La Royne Catherine de Medicis 1554", exquisitely enameled on metal, are framed in formal black and gold.

Home of J. B. Johnson

An open terrace inviting relaxation. Couches of moss-green plastic and leather covered Jalisco chairs provide for lounging, while the soft trickle of water in the fountain's pool is a happy foil to the street sounds below.

Back of the curtains is a small, self-contained apartment in white and greens. The bookshelves, beside a starkly plain corner fireplace, have a background of Indian bark paintings from Guerrero. A small, wooden, Yalalag figure, Porfirio Díaz in his younger days with gun in hand, guards the room, which is dominated by the old *santo*, stripped of paint except for his flesh colored hands and face.

Part of a heavy lintel supported on carved corbels is a shelf for small copper pitchers and a large Tarascan plate. This inglenook, reminiscent of the cherished recess by the fire in an old English home, has been produced to give balance to the living room which a small corner fireplace would fail to do.

A Metepec conception in pottery of the sun. Purple, yellow, aquamarine, deep red eyes, orange eyebrows, and a shocking-pink mustache, all below an ostentatious display of gold, make this plaque a terrific riot of color.

Museo Nacional de Artes e Industrias Populares

The charming Évora *pousada*, a former convent, has a tester bed in its "President's Room"; made of ebony, a Portuguese design sometimes found in México. The fine wood turnings of the posts and spindles are accented by molded brass collars, while a web-work of pierced-brass ornaments the flat members of the head.

Casa Raimoro is one of the many white-washed houses in Ronda, a very old city seemingly suspended between earth and sky among the mountains above Torremolinos, Spain. This early home is maintained as a local museum. In one room, a twisted-post bed of the 17th century, covered with an Arabic embroidered throw, backs against a heavy, damask hanging. In addition to the central, small ivory *santo*, some of the incised mouldings of the intricately carved head are accented with ivory.

192   Crisp simplicity: white *cambaya* draperies against white walls with contrasting crown, headboard and curtain hold-backs of wood, carved and deeply stained.

Under the hearth, logs are conveniently tucked to enhance the living ease of a calm room.

A fascinating collage in high key by Lucile Wilkinson hangs on the tapering chimney breast.

Home of John and Emily Haugh

Two tall tin candlesticks with white oval shades flank the arched colonnade of the headboard. Robust, turned posts carry a moss-green tester fringe above a moss-green bedspread. The double chest with pierced lock escutcheons completes the feeling of age which distinguishes this former Post House.

Home of David M. and Anne Wilson

Although beds now seem less important as decorative pieces, the reverse is true in contemporary México. Seldom foot boards, but the treatment of the headings often approaches the regal. Here, a carved and pierced headboard has a background of tasseled hangings in greenish-blue *cambaya*.

195

One of the happy features accompanying the rebirth of an old home as Mérida's new hotel, *Casa del Balam,* is the clean informality of its modern decorations. In a typical bedroom of ample size, twin headboards stained a dark brown support well designed pieces of contemporary iron work against a white wall.

A cut-out of flat iron depicting the details of Christ's suffering on the Cross, is customarily placed in a prominent spot on new construction in Ecuador; a symbol of protection for the building crafts.

Home of Robert F. Whitehouse

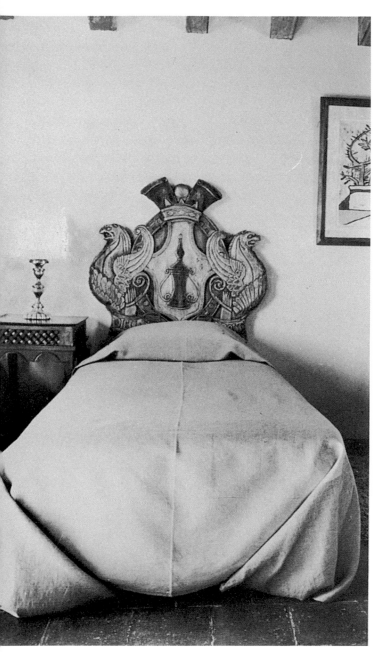

One of twin headboards in a guest room of the home-on-the-hill above Villa Montaña which Ray Coté has been remodeling. This headboard, from San Miguel de Allende, is remindful of the magic in the products of Jeanne Valentine.

Home of Paul Barnes

A bedspread in stripes of yellow, tan and browns leads you to a flamboyant, carved headboard, originally a curtain valance. Light for reading is concealed behind the curved, wood apron carrying the marble shelf of a former console. The Metepec candle holder is included just in case the local electricity falters.

Above a red dado the wall behind twin beds uses a novel treatment of stretched textile, corresponding with the bed covering—red and green posies on a field of white. Red bolsters, bright brass bed heads, gold framed Godey prints, all over a black fur rug, make a gay bedroom.

Handsome *ramilletes* in brass: above the cast urn with its elegant handles, the shield, repoussé in flowers, grapes, and leaves, is further enriched by free-standing wheat and more flowers.

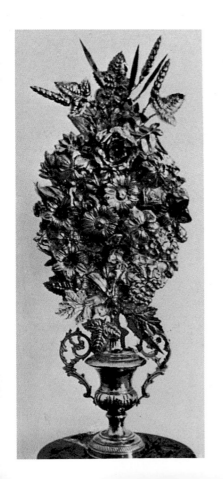

Home of Frances Stoddard

Former *cancelas* are used to advantage as backgrounds for a combination of mattress and box springs; they lend elegance to an otherwise ordinary treatment. Here, the entire closure after removal from its original setting is used. Within the transom and two side panels the pair of spindled doors hang free, 76 inches wide and 114½ inches high over-all.

Home of Ray Coté

A Victorian mahogany crib 57 inches high is suspended between two turned posts rigidly held upright by wide, spreading feet; safely and easily rockable. With embroidered lawn curtains held by dull lavender bows, this swinging cradle is a charmer.

A coquettish young lady, unquestionably a "doll", is robust with color. "Vivi", designed by Billie Bisgaard has a lissome body of sponge rubber with articulated legs. Dressed in a pink print, her big eyes beam at you from under a carefully tied hair-do of bright yellow yarn. Her constant companion is the little mouse (right).

Some of the many tin fantasies created by the José Velasco family of Oaxaca. This brilliantly hued band, commanded by the officer on a high-stepping steed, is complete with an emblazoned, waving banner and its color guard.

In Mérida, the dining room of the Pedro M. Peon de Regil home is enclosed yet open; double doors in two walls and a wide grille in the third. The fourth is honored by the portrait of an ancestor whose daughter married a Señor Peon, the first member of his family in Yucatán. Below a glazed pottery pitcher bears the Peon coat-of-arms.

Home of Pedro and Lia Ponce

Below a ceiling of dark charcoal-blue, this limestone chimney forms the lower landing wall of the stairs on the following pages. Artifacts from Pátzcuaro, Uxmal and Tonalá naïvely edge the hearth. At the left, the peach walls of an alcove are pictured-covered, while below and opposite, a varied group of crucifixes, some small and some minute, enhance a library wall.

203

Starting opposite the main entrance door of a recently constructed home, the wide and inviting flight of stairs typifies the grace of Yucatán living in Mérida.

Home of Pedro and Lia Ponce

Under the flying terrazzo stairs opposite, a garden of potted plants surround a
more than ample bird cage with its two towers enlivened by paper flowers.

In the guest house a handsomely moulded brass finial supplements an ornate design of scrolls and leaves in forged iron forming the starter newel for runs of unusual balusters, square bars ending in "C" scrolls.

Home of David M. and Anne Wilson

206

The stair wall of the main house is most impressive with this shell-headed niche and urn, so typical of the Italian Renaissance. Actually it is an ingenious trompe de l' oeil painted by John Beadle.

Home of David M. and Anne Wilson

A gracefully curving masonry staircase with exceptional finesse uses an elegant design in flat iron and small, square members to support the sweeping rail.

Home of Jean-Paul Olivier

Below, a modern *reja* gives decorative interest to the metal-shuttered, ground-floor window of a Seville home. The grille of ¼ inch by 1¼ inch flat iron bars, halved and tied with beaded rings at the intersections, is bordered by double "C" scrolls.

Above, a *reja* overlooking the main stair of the *Alcázar*, Seville. Delicately wrought spindles in two tiers, separated by an embossed horizontal member support a magnificent cresting of naturalistic motifs, conventionalized with features adaptable to architectural usage.

209

On the remains of the substantial demolition of a pseudo-Spanish residence of the 1900's, the Oliviers have built a new home, distinctively French in character. The detail of one of the several balcony railings is shown below. It follows the fine pattern on Page 208 in its delineation of the pineapple, for years a symbol of hospitality.

in

apricot

and

fern green

A residence in the Pedregal de San Angel is particularly noteworthy for its distinguished doors. The inner panels of this unusual pair leading from the atrium to the library, were found in Celaya. Later, moldings and incised bottom panels, repeating the background design of the old above were added as required to fit the opening. On each leaf, two apostles in low relief are above and below a *santa* in very deep relief, partially free-standing: on the right Luke and Matthew and on the left, John and Mark.

At top, an antique, delicate carving in wood of a vase and flowers, 62 inches high, is mounted and painted a goldish bronze.

Home of Joseph and Viola Turner

Walls of the *estancia* in tones of apricot, repeated throughout the home, are here tempered by cool, fern-green of the iron furniture with apricot and green velvet cushions, green shag rug and variegated green leaves of potted plants.

A glimpse of the *sala* with its elaborately carved golden mantel, a sienna-colored marble facing flanked by 18th century *estípites*. The curving chimney breast, decorated with a graceful plaster motif, disappears through the timbered ceiling.

Exquisitely turned spindles and carved scroll-work of these doors with fixed side panels, now between the *estancia* and *comedor*, formerly screened an arched opening with the circular transom on the following page.

A wall with apricot tints in the sunlight, a golden aviary and beige sandstone columns form the background of this dramatic *comedor*. The central arched ceiling whose sides are enriched by plaster traceries of grape vines, separates the twin dining groups.

In a shallow recess of the *tepetate* wall, an enchanting cage is tenanted by two white cockatoos from Singapore. Simple vertical bars are crowned by an elaborate, mushroom-shaped dome, pierced to repeat the grape motif of the arched ceiling.

Finely executed and finished, these partial copies of the entrance doors to the former Bishop's Palace in Oaxaca were carved on the site by a Puebla *maestro*, a handsome example of shallow, incised carving.

Home of Joseph and Viola Turner

Ceilings typical of Spanish construction in the 14th century.

Opposite, the ceiling of the dining room in a stately *parador* formerly the Palacio de Los Condes de Oropesa. Between the rafters, whose soffits are molded, are a series of panels painted with a repetitive design now barely distinguishable.

Above, a magnificently restored ceiling of the *Alcázar* in Seville is evidence of the brilliance of the Moorish occupation. The intricate design formed by the members supporting the horizontal surface is superb.

219

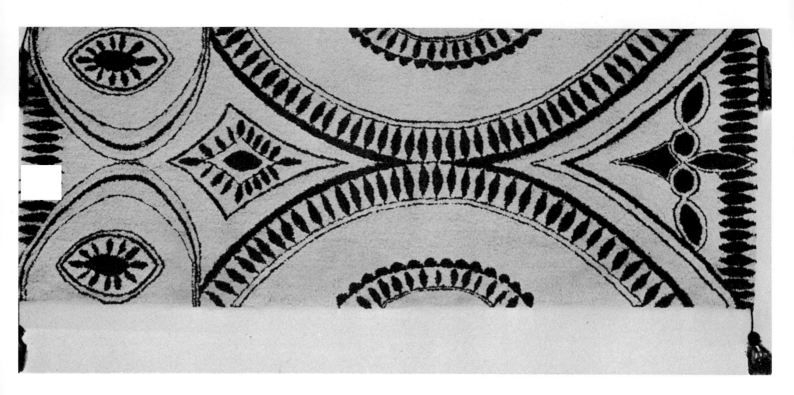

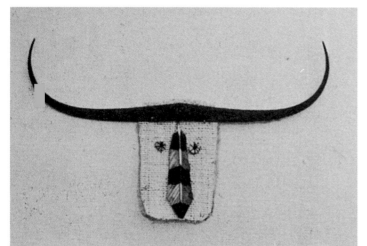

Heavy wool rugs about 77 inches long, woven on hand looms are examples of the design skill of Cynthia Sargent. Above, patterns in intense blue and lavender on whitened wool while below, black motifs and tassels are on native white.

Left: Open calipers, bit of sisal cloth, an odd feather and two jade beads combine to picture a "Borisov" Texas longhorn.

Saul Borisov asks what one sees upon encountering a tiger. Above, his woven answer in natural wool; masses of blackish stripes, an expectant red tongue, and then if still unchewed, the animal's full face.

A lion of many colors on a background of pink and orange outlined in woven black yarn. The pensive jungle king in blues with a green belly has dull gold, penetrating eyes.

With varied materials, textures and imaginative subjects, Borisov's loomings are always stimulating.

Portrait of a boy wearing a newspaper hat, playing a hardened *bandido*. Except for the cut-out mask of sisal on a background of streaked blues, the wool colors vary from brown hair, to shaded blue eyes and features outlined in red.

Here is a corner in the display rooms of Sarita's Sala de Artes. Suspended groupings of chartreuse-painted metal cubes cast a yellowish light over the couches, paper flowers and a noisy, woolen rooster.

A British-French alliance

Overlooking San Miguel de Allende from its easterly mountain slope, formal, pink *cantera* piers carry double entrance gates of dainty, diagonal iron members antiqued to greenish-gray.

Opposite, characters from Jeanne Valentine Schlee's *taller*; a Colonial British officer and a rugged, London Tower "Beefeater". Both in papier-mâché, with richly colored costumes of the periods, are here as companions of their countryman, Charles G. Schlee.

Home of Charles G. and Jeanne Valentine Schlee

From the main entrance, out of view at the far left, stairs behind wood and iron screening lead to the 2nd floor and its balustraded organ loft. The chimney wall in pink with deeper shades of pinkish-gray stone rises some 22 feet above the rich, brown tile floor to the timbered ceiling.

Incorporating certain air-circulation features in its construction, this fireplace is designed as a compliment to Mr. Schlee's homeland. The stone lions, although seemingly a bit contented with their little crowns, recall their rampant ancestor of the British coat-of-arms.

Up some steps from the *sala*, the dining area fireplace might well be in rural France. The ample semi-circular firebox, ending in narrow brick jambs, supports a traditionally high mantel over a knee-high hearth. Blue and green designs on white tile sparkle across the frieze. A deep copper apron, edged in stepped scallops, adds to the homeyness as well as serving a practical purpose.

On the preceding page, a storage recess in a working kitchen with walls of oatmeal colored tiles and red brick. Fruit motifs designed by Mrs. Schlee are applied to the mossy-green cabinet and interspersed on the pearly wainscot. The fan-like iron grille does double duty, both decorative and practical.

A superior, worldy-wise cat is another imaginative creation from the Jeanne Valentine workshop. Made of papier-mâché, she is 21½ inches to the tips of her ears. A seductive red mouth with gold whiskers ending in curlicues, is below cool, green eyes under pink eyelids. And with a bright gold knotted scarf, green hearts outlined in scrolls of gold painted string, she is really a grande dame.

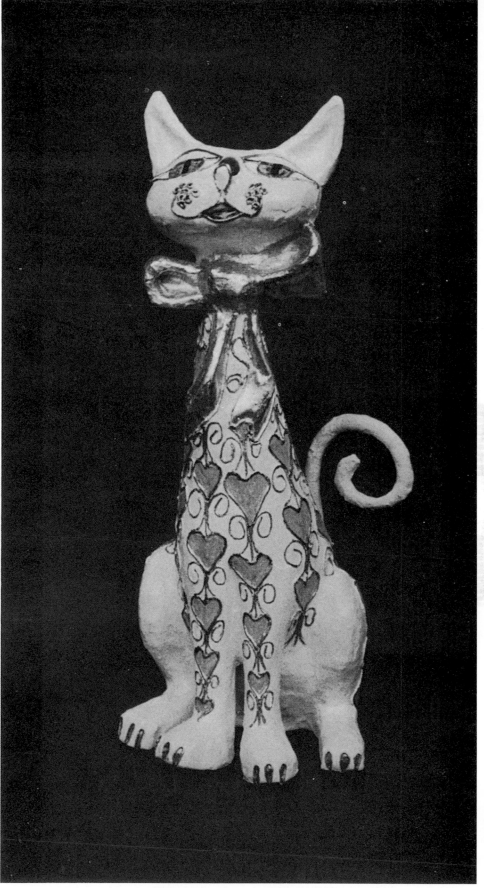

Home of Charles G. and Jeanne Valentine Schlee

229

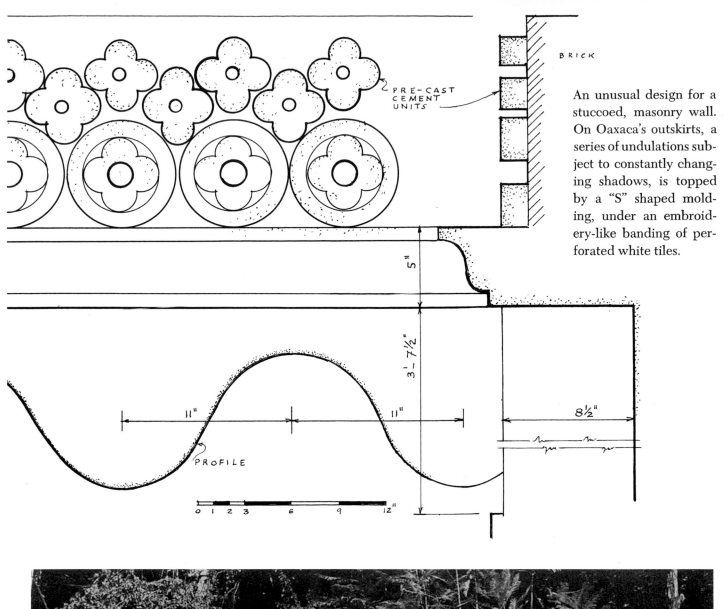

BRICK

PRE-CAST
CEMENT
UNITS

An unusual design for a stuccoed, masonry wall. On Oaxaca's outskirts, a series of undulations subject to constantly changing shadows, is topped by a "S" shaped molding, under an embroidery-like banding of perforated white tiles.

5"

3'—7½"

11"   11"

PROFILE

8½"

0 1 2 3   6   9   12"

An entrance to the quadrangle fronting the former Portuguese royal palace, now a part of the University in Coimbra. Flowing rounded steps lead to twin flights beyond the heavy, forged iron gates. Centered on the gray-to-black, weather-stained walls, an abbreviated broken pediment is flanked by finials. The crowned figure in wind-swept robes stands on a carved base above a rectangular plaque with the words SAPIENTA ÆDENCAVIT.

doves for Peace
pineapples for Hospitality

Simple doors of weathered planks secured with eight-leaf bosses and daisy headed studs, in a rough rubble wall, accentuate an inviting *cantera* surround. The relatively deep-relief carving describes the owners, Dr. Virgilio Fernandez and Gene Byron de Fernandez, designed by Gene Byron — doves for peace and pineapples for hospitality.

Opposite, an example of artistry in ceramics, only one of her varied talents. This seductive dancer in chocolate-brown, carrying a large pottery bowl, is decorated with a bird in earth-red and yellow and floral designs of greens with yellow blossoms.

In homes built on the old *hacienda* walls of Marfil, the expected is seldom found. Upon entering, two massive stone arches seem to stride ahead as they separate the reception area from the *sala*, each with curved brick ceilings. The effect is breath-taking.

Below, a chest from Celaya on the far wall has interesting gouged floral patterns on its doors. It carries, with other craft objects, two "Gene Byron" lamp standards in old avocado and gold.

Between *sala* and *comedor* the iron stair opposite, found in a demolition yard, is one of several ways to reach the upper floor.

The pineapple motif appears again on both the hearth-riser and the 12 feet long *cantera* frieze of the *sala's* wide-spreading firehood.

An arched recess — wood shelves mostly filled with Michoacán ceramics — is between a long braid of garlic and a pineapple shaped cutting board. Fanciful inserts in dark blues, greens and burgundies, all designed by Gene Byron, decorate the tiled *brasero*.

Home of Dr. Virgilio Fernandez and Gene Byron de Fernandez

Home of Dr. Virgilio Fernandez and Gene Byron de Fernandez

The town of Marfil lies at the entrance to the gorge through which the Guanajuato
River flows to the west. In 1905 a disastrous flood left nothing but a mass of silted
ruins, the former ore-reduction *haciendas.* Reconstructed as above, the old walls
are now parts of unusual homes.

237

In earlier days, Mexican *piñatas* had one primary purpose, a colorful repository for goodies which could be broken with one whack of a stick. Then the surrounding party would scramble for the shower of candies, trinkets, etc., which tumbled over the blindfolded whacker's head. Now, many *piñatas* are for decoration only as is this white, frilled-paper lion with gilded toes and roguish, black eye lashes on a mask of gold.

Some natives of Yalalag, a town high in the hills east of Oaxaca, are especially adept in the carving and coloring of ingenuous wooden subjects. Below, a happy lion, 18 inches long, nibbles a mango, unconcerned by the glowering jaguar in the background. Overhead hang tin Christmas ornaments, "Mad Things", painted in violent colors.

Home of José Trinidad Muñoz Rivera   *Yalalag*

Villa Montaña

In *Centro Regional de las Artesanias Y el Folklore*, Puebla, a wood dance mask patterned in black on yellow, has bristly whiskers and a red leather tongue — a terrifying ensemble.

A crude counterpart of the early Tarascan *troje* porch columns. It is of particular interest, however, because of the imaginative inclusion of a raised face, an angel, on the inner core of its structural member.

240

Mérida, near the tip of the Yucatán peninsula, leaves architecturally an indelible impression which differs markedly from other Mexican communities. Partially isolated from its mainland due to former transport difficulties, this old city, founded in 1542, resembles a richly woven tapestry of diverse cultures. Demure thatched houses are scattered between those of more sophistication with each maintaining its innate dignity.

Predominately French in influence, Mérida stresses pilastered façades treated light-heartedly, such as those of the Louis-Phillipe era. French windows protected by *rejas* which hug the walls because of narrow sidewalks, are made of delicate strap-iron members, some twisted, frequently tied with lead rosettes.

A truly regal *palapa* graces the beach of Formentor, Majorca. Heavy with grasses the crown-like mass of loops above a fuzzy ruching is topped by a high and mighty panache.

In the garden of Hotel Hacienda Uxmal, a thatched roof *cabaña* is a workshop for local artisans. The moonfaced, multiflowered cat gains distinction by standing while the brilliantly bordered overdresses of the musical angels are typical costumes of Yucatán.

This *patio* in a former Mérida home of the late Fernando Barbachano is the core of a new hotel named in his honor, Casa del Balam, "house of the tiger" or "chair on which the leading tiger would sit". The design of these arches was influenced, no doubt, by others of earlier construction similar to those on the following page. Below, is the sharply defined arcade of the sacristy adjoining the old church of San Juan, while above, the more flowing arches enclose the front loggia of Hacienda San Pedro on Mérida's outskirts. Both are inspirational examples of the Arabic influence carried over from Spain.

Portion of the marvelous, ornamental band or freize which girdles the structure forming the easterly side of El *Cuadrángulo de las Monjas*, Uxmal. This limited section of the colossal group of partially reconstructed Mayan ruins, said to have been founded in 1007 A.D., is an example of the intricate carvings and mosaics which were repeated with other motifs throughout a most impressive, pre-Hispanic city.

The National Museum of Anthropology is world renowned. Above one of the long parallel side walls forming the magnificent *patio* with its simulated Rain Forest. Hollow, rectangular sections of aluminum, similar but alternating in the positioning of the vertical sections, form in mass an extraordinary grille-work; a schematic representation of serpents so favored in Mayan ornamentation.

In the fascinating book, *Design Motifs of Ancient México* by Jorge Enciso, is included the pre-Hispanic flat stamp opposite as well as the simpler ones, a Humming Bird and a Frog, on previous pages. Found in Cempoala, Veracruz, this bird is said to pattern a Road-runner or a Shouting Pheasant.

Aluminum with varied weather resistant finishes is widely used for trim and frame material on Mexico's new, multi-floored buildings. Below is an ingenious design screening a moderate sized opening. The repetitive use of sections, 13 inches long, all identical, produces an unusual loose knit effect in steel-gray.

Calle Rio Rhin 77, México D.F.

Photograph by Foto Rivas

A ceramic of around the 7th century from the Mitla collection of Howard Leigh. A bat with a human head inside its open mouth carries an incense bowl used in religious ceremonies. According to Mr. Leigh, the Zapotecs were the only tribe to model bats in their pottery. These findings from early civilizations will continue to be exciting forerunners for the brilliant future of today's México.